The Little Book Of Daily Sunshine

Bite-Sized Inspiration To Light Up Your Day

D1487925

By
Clare Josa

Whether you just want to start the day with a smile on your face or be inspired to change your life, The Little Book Of Daily Sunshine fits the bill. Titbits of deep thought; bursts of rainbow thinking; flashes of heart opening clarity, it has it all. Give it a try, it'll brighten every day and it might just change your life (it has for me!) Make every day brighter.

Pendella Buchanan

Author of Layers

I have been enjoying a dose of "Daily Sunshine" for the past four months. Many of the messages have had an impact on me but none more than the one I read today. I now realise that I have been looking for happiness in all the wrong places. Yeah, sure I've read that happiness comes from within, but this has hit home with me "BIG TIME". Thank You, Thank You, Thank You........

Janelle

I love my Daily Sunshine messages! They're exactly the thing that is needed to jolt me out of early-morning-grumpy mode every day and make me think about what makes me and others happy. Thank you for them and bless you.

Catriona

I love reading these messages. Sometimes I am having a difficult day I read a message and I have a breath of fresh air.

Autumn

This little book does exactly what it says on the cover, it provides you with a dose of Daily Sunshine, no matter what the weather is like outside. I've been reading Clare's Daily Sunshine messages over the past years and they have been a great help through some difficult and stressful times: to cope with the falling out of husband and son without appearing to take sides; to maintain patience and hope during a very long and difficult house sale; to conserve and build the strength required to pack and move house; to keep smiling when things don't go right. Thank you Clare.

Joy

I really appreciate the way the Daily Sunshine messages take me out of my head and into my present-moment experience of life. Sometimes when I'm lost in all the things I do, I read a Daily Sunshine message and it helps me re-focus on what's important – on what matters; and that's rarely the 'to do' list. It brings me back to 'real life'.

Peter

Published by Beyond Alchemy Publishing 2012
For bulk orders contact hello@beyond-alchemy.com

© Clare Josa 2012

ISBN 978-1908854407

Cover design by Gétha Goosen

The advice in this book is intended for educational purposes only and it is not intended to substitute for professional medical advice. In the event that you use any of this information for yourself, the publisher and author accept no responsibility for your actions. Always consult your medical professional, if you are unsure about whether any of the suggested techniques are suitable for you.

Table Of Contents

Dedication

With love to Luigi-san, Tigger and Raffster.

May you laugh your way through life and may your inner radiance light up the world.

Gratitude And Acknowledgements

A huge thank you to everyone who has helped to create *The Little Book Of Daily Sunshine*.

To those of you who received the daily emails over the past five years, a huge thank you for going and using this stuff! Thank you also for the questions you asked, which taught me more than you could imagine.

Thank you to all who have supported and encouraged me throughout this project: especially those of you on Facebook, who have been my virtual cheerleaders, and to my family, for accepting and forgiving all the times I scuttled away to send more Daily Sunshine messages to the world.

And finally, thank you to you, for choosing to allow these messages to help you make shifts in your life. Your 'future self' will thank you for it.

My deepest wish is that you will feel inspired to move past old blocks, limiting beliefs and excuses, creating the life you have been dreaming of, falling in love with the wondrous being that is your true self.

With love, Namaste,

Clare. ♡

www.ClareJosa.com

Bonus Gifts
Join The Readers' Club Now

As a thank you for reading *The Little Book Of Daily Sunshine*, there are bonus gifts waiting for you at the Daily Sunshine website, including:

- a 20 minute Daily Sunshine Deep Relaxation MP3 audio

- beautiful photographs with key quotes from the book, for you to share with your friends, to use as your computer screen-saver or to print out and inspire you

- membership of *The Little Book Of Daily Sunshine* readers-only area in our forum

- a monthly email newsletter, packed with inspirational articles, expert strategies and subscriber-only competitions

To claim your bonus gifts, please register at:

www.DailySunshine.co.uk/bonus

How To Get The Most From This Book

The Little Book Of Daily Sunshine is designed to work for you, however you want to use it. It has been intentionally designed in a pocket-sized format, to allow you to take it with you, whenever you want some extra inspiration to light up your day. The messages have been created to be succinct and quick to read, whilst still bringing you all you need in that moment, with the potential to change your life, if that's what you want.

- Some people like to read this book like a traditional book, from cover to cover.
- Others like to read a message each morning, to inspire their day.
- You might like to take a relaxing breath and ask yourself, "What do I most need to hear, right now?" before opening the book at random. It's funny how often it is spot on.

However you choose to read it, the most important thing is to gently open your mind and heart to let the messages weave their magic. Ask yourself the question from each message and let your inner wisdom give you the answers you have been looking for. And above all, enjoy the journey!

Daily Sunshine Messages

A beautiful diamond asks to be viewed from many angles, shining in the light.

When we look at a sparkling gem, we don't just view it from one position. We pick it up and turn it round, to see how it reflects the light from every angle.

The same goes for inspiration in life.

It calls us to pick it up, to view it from many angles; to try it on for size; to apply it to different situations. It asks us to shine our light on it, to see how it might lift us today. And, if we encounter it again in the future, it asks us to look at it with fresh eyes, to see if there are deeper levels in there for us.

When life lessons come back to you or inspiration strikes twice, it's your deeper wisdom's unsubtle hint that there is still more for you to learn; other facets and sparkles to experience.

Don't dismiss it, just because you think you already know it. On this beautiful journey of life, there is always another perspective to enjoy.

Is there another way you could look at things today

The second best time to plant an oak tree is today.

It's easy to have regrets about not having started an important project sooner.

We all have projects, dreams and ideas that would have benefited from a decade or more of our loving, inspired attention and action.

We can't change the past.

But that doesn't mean we have to despair. We can do something about it today.

All our power and choice lies in the present moment – right here and now.

The choices we make today create the future that we are dreaming of.

And taking action on those choices is what will get that oak tree started. It's never too late to make a start.

What action could you take today, to start planting that oak tree?

There is always enough. It might not arrive in the way you're expecting, but there is always enough.

With all the talk of the credit crunch and financial crises, it's no wonder our culture is in a space of believing that there's not enough.

When we get fixated with not having enough; with lack; with things going wrong; then we're setting our mind's radar to spot more of that. We spot the chances to experience more 'not enough of'. We'll miss the wide open doors that could take us back into the world of 'enough'.

But there can be enough, if we let that 'enough' in. It's up to us to allow what we need to arrive in our experience of life. It's not just about money – it's about everything we need, including love and support. I'm not suggesting you should force yourself to believe that there is plenty, if that's not your current way of thinking.

But how about allowing yourself to move towards hoping that there might be enough; that things might improve?

If you focus on what you don't want, then that's where you'll keep steering your ship.

We tend to end up where we're looking. It's hard to safely turn a corner, while you're looking straight ahead. And birds never look behind them as they fly.

By keeping our attention on what's not to our liking, we end up getting more of it. It's like being at a buffet and concentrating so hard on how much you hate celery salad that you don't spot all of your favourite dishes right next to it.

What we don't want fills our thoughts and our conversations. "I don't want to mess up the presentation." "I don't want him to behave like that." We're usually trying to change or prevent things that are out of our control – outside of us.

If you're stuck on what you don't want, there's a magic question that can help you turn things around. It's a simple question that's pretty much guaranteed to change your life:

What do I want instead? Can you feel the difference?

Your thoughts impact your physical body and your health. Is it time to choose them with care?

Your thoughts produce chemical reactions in your body that alter your biology and trigger your emotions.

Happy thoughts set off happy chemical reactions and you'll feel good and so will your body. Sad thoughts set off a sad one and you'll feel bad.

Our habitual 'tone' of thoughts sets the baseline of our body's hormone responses, which impacts our biology and our health – physically, mentally and emotionally. Researchers are now proving connections between these processes and diseases So it's worth choosing wisely which thoughts to feed!

If you don't want a particular thought to trigger a chain reaction, lovingly let it go. To find a more uplifting thought, ask yourself:

Which thought could I choose right now that will lift my spirits – even just a little bit?

Fed up of feeling stressed? It's ok to turn that mountain back into a molehill. Here's how.

Feeling stressed seems to be an epidemic. Yet regular stress is playing havoc with our health, careers and even our closest relationships. If the stuff that's stressing you feels the size of a mountain, going round and round in your head, there's a simple technique you can use, to turn it back into a molehill: **Write it down.**

Write down your answers to the following questions to help stop the mental chatter and slow you down, reducing your stress levels.

- "What *specifically* is the problem?"
  This helps you get out of the drama and be clear about the issue.

- "What do I want instead?"
  This helps you see that there might just possibly be a light at the end of the tunnel.

- "Which single, baby step could I take, right now, to move towards what I want instead?"

By getting specific about what's up and breaking the solution down into chunks, you'll feel the overwhelm melt away.

It's ok to ask for help. We're not designed to 'do' life on our own.

As humans, we have a strong need for community and belonging. Yet, in our modern Western society, most of us try to struggle along, doing everything ourselves.

We have lost touch with our 'tribe' – our support network. It might be your extended family or it might be your friends, colleagues and neighbours.

As a culture, we have convinced ourselves that it's a sign of weakness, asking for help. And we tend to believe that asking for help would be imposing on others. But think about how you feel, when you get the chance to help someone else who needs your support? How about letting others feel that way, by being able to help you?

Knowing when you need support and asking for it isn't a sign of weakness. It takes courage and strength to open up to let others help you – but it will change your life.

Where do I need help and support today? How could I learn to accept that help?

You are not your behaviour. Your personality is just a set of clothes you wear when you're awake.

You are not what you do! I really struggle when I hear people make statements that put them in boxes: "I *am* an addict."; "I *am* co-dependent."; "I *am* bad at such-and-such." These are statements that apply a behaviour to us at the level of our identity – the core of our being.

You don't 'be' those things; you 'do' them. There's a world of difference. Things we 'do' can change.

Negative "I am" statements effectively close the door to the possibility of change or of having a choice. You are permanently wedding who you are to a behaviour. Is that what you really want?

We can choose how to behave. Habits can be changed. You are so much more than your habits!

And the first – and most important – step towards that change is to shift your language. Save "I am" for times when you really mean it!

Who do you want to be today?

Breathe deeply, choose your thoughts wisely, live in the moment, open your heart and accept yourself as the beautiful being that you are.

That's my five-part recipe for happiness and inner peace. Everything else is just glitter around the edges. All it takes is for us to set our intention. Inner peace is within your reach.

Breathing deeply is key for good health. We can all learn to choose to breathe deeply. **Choosing thoughts wisely** impacts our body, mind and soul. We can all learn to choose our thoughts. **Living in the moment** gives us back our power of choice, in every aspect of life. We can all learn to live in the present moment. **Opening your heart to loving and being loved** sets you free from most of life's stresses. We can all learn to live with the open-hearted innocence of a child. **Accepting yourself as the wonderful being you truly are** lets go of anxiety and most of our fears! We can all learn to accept ourselves, one moment at a time.

Which of these would you like to play with today?

If the door is closed, stop pushing it.

If the door seems to be closed, that's a sign to pause. Either you're trying to kick down the wrong door or the timing isn't yet right.

We all know the feeling: we need to get something done, but it keeps going wrong. Nothing seems to work out. It's as though the door is closed. But we keep trying to push our way through it.

The problem is that while we're trying to bust our way through closed doors we get so fixated with the direction we thought we were heading in that we miss the wide open door right next to it.

If you feel like you're having to force things, then you're most likely either off-course or off-timing.

Sometimes things don't happen the way we expect. Instead of keeping going, trying the same thing over and over, how about asking yourself:

Is there another door that's waiting for me to knock on it, right now?

Is it time to stop clinging to the past?

Our past is no longer real. All that's left of it is a collection of memories that represent those old events. Our experience of those situations is governed by the filters and beliefs that run in our minds, so they, too, are just an illustration – perhaps even an illusion – of what actually happened.

If you asked ten people to give you an account of an event, you would hear ten unique perspectives. We all interpret things differently.

So why do we cling to our past, as though it were the ultimate Truth? Why do we insist on hanging on to our history and letting it influence our present and our future? Why do we let it tell us who we can be and what we can achieve?

All of our power to make choices and create our future lies not in our past, though it might have lessons for us; it lies in the present moment.

We find it when we lovingly let go of living in the past.

To come back to the present, take a deep breath and tell yourself: "I am here." Feel the shift.

Life is too short to drink bad coffee.

Ok, so I'm not really talking about coffee. I'm talking about choices.

Imagine you make a choice, then you realise that it's not really what you wanted, after all. But we tend to keep on going in that direction, because we had made the choice – even if the coffee tastes awful.

All our choices – our actions – have consequences – outcomes. Whether the choice was as big as leaving a job or as seemingly small as a chain of thoughts, it is still a choice.

If you don't like the outcome of a choice, you can always do something about it. In fact, it's essential to do something about it. The only way you'll feel at peace is either to make another choice or to genuinely accept the outcome of the choice you made and to change your attitude towards it.

I'm not saying it's easy, but it will set you free from so much stress, anxiety and worry that surely it's worth the effort?

Is there a new choice you need to make today?

When your mind hears "I am..." it takes it as an instruction.

"I am" is your mind's unconscious instruction to run its pre-programmed auto-pilot scripts to match whatever comes after the 'am'. Whether the next word is lazy, happy, angry, rubbish, stupid, bad, tired or inspired, your mind dives into its old, well-rehearsed thoughts, feelings and actions, to match the instruction you gave.

"Ok, so that's the role we're playing today! Cool! I can handle that for you." says our unconscious mind. Imagine being on a diet while telling yourself, "I am fat," or studying for an exam while complaining, "I am stupid"?

The auto-pilot scripts mean we don't have to make conscious choices. But if we didn't really want to keep what is after the 'am', then it steals your freedom. The label keeps you stuck. Instead, it helps to get specific about the behaviour or event, talking about how you did or felt about something, rather than who you are. If you catch yourself at the "I am" trick, ask yourself - playfully:

Is that really who I want to be? No? Who am I?

Is it time to stop 'pretending to breathe'?

Most of us don't breathe properly. Stress, poor posture and sitting too much causes us to slouch. Your diaphragm can't move properly and the body resorts to upper-chest breathing, starving your body and brain of oxygen. This triggers the sympathetic nervous system's stress response, also making you tired and grumpy.

There's a huge difference between 'pretending to breathe' – breathing just enough to stay 'alive' – and breathing deeply enough to be 'living'.

Shallow upper-chest breathing is a common symptom of stress and poor posture. It's nothing more (usually) than a bad habit. But its impacts are many – poor blood oxygenation can lead to tiredness, grumpiness, fuzzy thinking and physical disease. Fortunately practising a few minutes of deep belly breathing each day can help you to develop healthy breathing habits that release tension, help you think more clearly, give you more energy and help you to concentrate, as well as improving your health.

Here's a 5 minute belly-breathing meditation that you might enjoy: www.DailySunshine.co.uk/bonus

It's easier to change the direction of a moving object than one that's rooted to the spot.

It doesn't matter whether you're moving in exactly the right direction or not. What matters is that you're moving. When we're stuck; standing still; it's hard for things to change. The longer we stay still, the more firmly we get rooted to the spot in our old, out-dated habits, thoughts, beliefs and environment. Once you're moving – making progress – it's easier to spot the shifts that are needed, to refine your route.

Staying flexible in everyday life makes the process of larger change much easier. You are less stuck in your routines and less attached to things being done in a certain way. It keeps you moving. Do something differently each day – it might be the order in which you brush your teeth; it could be changing your route to work; it could be shifting your morning rhythm. It doesn't matter what.

Is there somewhere in your life where taking the first step to get moving could set you free today?

If you can't say anything kind, how about saying nothing?

It can feel natural to want to retaliate if someone behaves badly towards us. Lashing out when we're feeling angry is easy. But unkind words and deeds come at a price. They don't really make us feel better, if we're honest with ourselves. They just create more conflict.

Making your point with compassion and understanding shows inner strength and promotes peace. Ironically, it's also the fastest way to move towards the outcome you are hoping for. Using kind words helps you to stay on track with this.

It opens the door to miraculous, inspired solutions, rather than feeding tension, anger and aggression. It's not about giving in. It's about choosing not to dance the angry dance, whilst standing your ground.

Is there an area of your life that could do with a kinder response today?

The only thing you need to do today is breathe. Everything else is optional.

No matter how many hoops we force ourselves to jump through each day, no matter how many 'shoulds' we sprinkle along our path, the only thing we genuinely *have* to do each day is breathe.

No matter how much we have conditioned ourselves to believe we have to do, think or say certain things, if we are really honest with ourselves, we always have the power to choose.

Everything else is optional – our choice – no matter what our mind tells us or how difficult that choice may feel.

Imagine a life where you get to choose everything you do, think and say? Yes, you guessed it, you're already living it. It might feel difficult at first, but the more you play with this, the easier it gets.

How might it cut your stress levels today if you were to focus on breathing and leave everything else to choice?

You'll never know, unless you take the chance.

Sometimes we're so set on how things 'should' be or where we 'think' they're going that we miss the real opportunities that are scattered along our path.

How many times do we let those opportunities pass us by? Often it's only with hindsight that we can even see that opportunity was there.

Our fears, excuses and limiting beliefs – our life-long conditioning – can encourage us to look the other way until the chance has passed us by.

It's ok to feel scared. But surely overcoming a little fear is worth it, to allow yourself to take the next step on your journey?

How about choosing to keep a look-out for every open door? And if that open door feels scary, how about asking the 'future you', who has already stepped through that door, for some moral support?

And how about asking yourself, despite what you might have been expecting:

Is this the chance I have been waiting for? Will my 'future me' thank me for taking it?

It's ok to surround yourself with people who bring out the best in you. Actually, it's essential.

If we spend time with people who drag us down and drain our energy, we feel demoralised. If we spend time with people who lift our spirits and help us to see the magic of who we really are, we can feel amazing – and achieve anything!

Who we hang around with was chosen by the 'old' us. And sometimes those relationships have run their course. Rather than clinging to them, it's ok to create space. The friendship might fade away or blossom into something even better.

No matter how difficult it might seem, we can choose who to spend time with – and who we need a break from. And if you genuinely feel you can't say no, you could imagine a ball of light surrounding you when you're with that person, so that their draining energy doesn't have as much impact on you. It's a way of setting boundaries. Your future self will thank you for those choices.

Is there a boundary that could do with being made clearer today?

If you THINK before you speak, it might just change your world.

T   Is it truthful?

H   Is it helpful?

I   Is it important?

N   Is it necessary?

K   Is it kind?

Imagine applying these five short questions as a mantra, before you speak, in difficult situations? Yes, it takes practice. But how often might it change what you were going to say?

Just imagine how it could shift your personal and professional relationships? And how much conflict and stress it could prevent?

And how might it change things, if you were to apply it to the way you talk to yourself, too?

Hitting your comfort zone's boundaries is simply a sign that you're about to have the chance to grow.

We're not here on this Earth to stay still and stagnate. It's the nature of all living things to grow and change.

Think about the times when you have broken through old comfort zones – from learning to walk and talk to driving a car and every other skill you have ever acquired; every habit you have changed; every belief you have shifted.

You can stretch your comfort zones, gently but firmly. You don't have to shatter them or make it feel scary. You have stretched your old comfort zones over and over in the past. And you know how to ask for help and support, if you need it.

It's only as difficult and daunting as you tell yourself it's will be. How about making it easy?

How about imagining that comfort zone gently stretching and expanding by even just 5% today? Does that feel easier?

Everything is connected. Is it time to say thank you?

Everything is connected. Everything impacts the other elements in its system.

Somewhere out there, a tree is tirelessly creating oxygen, to allow you to breathe.

Somewhere out there, a rock is filtering water, to allow you to drink.

Somewhere out there, a river is flowing and a spring is bubbling, to bring you water.

Somewhere out there, the soil is teaming with microbes, to help grow the plants that will feed you.

Somewhere out there, the sunshine is shining – even behind the clouds – to help lift your spirits.

Somewhere out there, loved ones are waiting to support you.

Somewhere out there, your deeper wisdom is patiently waiting for you to check in with it.

Isn't it amazing?

For free daily gratitude emails & inspirational resources, visit www.MiracleOfGratitude.com

What could you choose to feel grateful for today?

Even when it's raining, the sunshine is still there.

The sunshine never goes anywhere – it just gets hidden by the clouds.

But clouds aren't solid. They are made of tiny moisture droplets that are constantly moving and changing. So they let the sun through between the gaps. All we need to do is to choose to feel it and see its effects.

The same goes for our inner peace and happiness or the love and support of those dear to us. It never leaves us. It's just that we get into the habit of obscuring it with clouds of other emotions. And we even fool ourselves into believing that it has 'gone away'.

But all we have to do, to catch sight of it again, is to choose a happier-feeling thought and to open our hearts to allow love and support to reach us. That's when the miracle happens and the clouds start to disperse.

That sunshine is inside you, all day, every day.

Is it time to let your inner sunshine out to play today?

When your mind creates a problem, your heart holds the answer. All problems are created by your mind.

Whatever is happening in life – no matter how wonderful or difficult it seems – our mind tells us how to experience it.

If we feel trapped in a situation, it's because our mind tells us it is so. If we feel hurt by someone's actions, it is because our mind tells us we should be. If we feel unlucky over an outcome, it is because our mind tells us we are. Our mind decides whether or not to turn the experience into a problem.

When we connect with our heart, we quieten down the mind's 'story' and 'drama', opening up the possibility of connecting with a deeper wisdom. It's our heart that offers us the chance to create solutions that are for the highest good of all involved, that lead to peace and happiness, that are created from love, not fear.

What message does your heart most want you to hear today?

10 Happiness Secrets That Children Would Love Us To Learn

Children can be our greatest teachers. And they remember so much more than we do about how to feel happy – and how to be who we really are. Here are 10 secrets to happiness that they'd like to share with you:

1. Ask for what you want.
   It's ok to be honest about our needs and desires.

2. Say what you're thinking.
   Of course, use compassion. But there's no point lying.

3. Cry, if you want to.
   Let those emotions out. Then let go and move on.

4. Wear your wellies, if you want to.
   It's ok to express who you really are, through what you're wearing. And jumping in puddles is fun!

5. Don't care what anyone else thinks.
   As long as your conscience lets you sleep at night, be who you are. It's what you're here for.

6. Spend time with those you love.
   Prioritise time with loved ones over all other activities. Life is too precious to put our 'to do' list and projected obligations ahead of those we love.

7. Tell silly jokes.
   Laughter is an essential element of a happy, healthy life. You might as well initiate it!

8. Get creative.

   Doing things with your hands – making things – gets you out of your thinking head and back into the present moment. It can relieve stress and help you miraculously spot solutions to problems that previously felt impossible.

9. If at first you don't succeed…

   Keep tweaking what you're doing until it works. Never give up on your dreams.

10. Go and pick a daisy.

   Stopping to admire a sunset or marvel at the beauty of a tiny daisy can help us get things back into perspective, feeling happier, fast.

If you could ask you inner child, right now, I'm wondering what he or she would like to tell you about how to feel happy?

Your unconscious mind can't understand a negative.

To understand the instruction "Don't mess it up!", your mind first has to imagine "Mess it up!", before it adds the "not".

Need convincing?

Right now: **don't** *think of a blue donkey climbing a prickly purple tree with a barking dog at the bottom of the trunk.*

What happened? Yup. You had to imagine it, before you got the 'not'.

It is how the mind works.

All those times when we're talking about what we don't want, guess what we have to imagine first? And that imagining triggers off the same emotions and physical reactions in your body as if it were actually happening.

It also triggers the mind's auto-pilot programmes for achieving the thing you don't want, with the "not" getting lost in the footnotes. And you can guess where that will lead.

The next time you spot yourself doing this, how about asking yourself:

"What do I want instead?"

Just because you couldn't, it doesn't mean you can't.

We grow and change over time. But our out-dated beliefs about what we can achieve risk keeping us stuck. When we experience not being able to do something, our mind generalises that experience and tells us it was so, it is so and it will continue to be so. If we believe that story, it will become our Truth.

We limit our dreams by what we *think* we can do. So we miss out on what we're truly here to do – and capable of achieving. But how about allowing yourself to hope? How about opening up to the possibility that the past doesn't have to rule your present and your future?

Just because it didn't work out last time, it doesn't mean it won't go well today – or tomorrow – or next month – or next year. You have grown and learned new ways of experiencing life since then.

You have changed since that last time. You are not that person any more. New outcomes aren't just possible – they're inevitable.

What if, one day, it might be possible? How might that change your actions today?

Acts of kindness come from the heart. They sow seeds of love along your path.

A true act of kindness has no attachment to receiving anything in return – not even a thank you. It has no agenda. It has no expectation of reward or recognition.

When kind acts are performed in this way, they are filled with love – for others and yourself.

And they can spread their magic far and wide.

True kindness has balance. It's not about martyring yourself. It's not about giving too much. It's not about ignoring your own needs. It's not about giving in order to get what you need, whether from the other person or from The Universe.

It's simply about thinking kind thoughts. And kind actions will automatically follow.

Like a boomerang, that kindness will come back to you. But it might not be in the way you expect. Keep your eyes open for it when the love along your path bears fruit.

Where you could share kindness today?

How tasting your tea can cut your stress levels.

Do you ever get to the end of a cup of tea with no recollection of drinking it? Or do you find yourself drinking your tea, whilst thinking about everything else you have to do? Does that actually get any of it done?

The next time you make yourself a drink (hot, cold, it doesn't matter), I invite you to taste it! It brings you back to the present moment and can cut your stress levels. Be completely aware of and fully present to the experience of 'tasting your tea'.

1. Sit down with your tea.
2. Before you pick it up and drink it, actually look at it.
3. Pick it up and notice the feel of the cup.
4. Before you drink the drink, take a sniff and allow yourself to notice the aroma.
5. As you start to drink, sipping gently or gulping, it's up to you, allow yourself to really taste your drink.
6. And, as you swallow, allow yourself to hear the sounds.

How do you feel, having tasted your tea?

Is it time to let go of your 'stuff'?

How many excuses do we make about not being able to let go of the past? How often do we defend our stories and insist on letting them fill our present and our future?

Our 'stuff' might be physical things from the past or mental and emotional 'baggage' that we loyally carry with us, every moment of every day. It can have a tendency to get in the way of the choices we could make, in our present moment, to create a new future. It keeps us stuck.

But, in any instant, we can choose to set ourselves free from that old stuff.

If you make the decision to let it go and lovingly see the invisible ties being released, it will be gone.

What would it take for you to choose, right now, to lovingly let go of the old stories; to turn to a fresh page to write a new one?

How about asking yourself the question:

Do I really want to carry that old story forward, forever, or am I ready to gently let it go today?

Our biggest addiction? Thinking. It has more impact on our experience of life than anything else we do.

We might think we're addicted to cigarettes, alcohol, caffeine or something else, but no physical world addiction could exist if we weren't already thinking the thoughts that created the environment to nurture those behaviours.

Each action starts with a thought – even if we're not consciously aware of it. Each habit starts with a single action, which is repeated often enough to become a habit. Each addiction starts with a habit.

So it all starts with thinking. And most of us are addicted to thinking.

Want to break a habit or make changes in your life? Then it's time to start with your thoughts. We can choose other thoughts by releasing those that no longer serve our highest good, one thought at a time. Is it time to let them go?

Are there any thought habits that are no longer serving you?

Is it time to start choosing your thoughts with more care? And yes, we CAN choose our thoughts.

We have trained ourselves, over the decades, to use our thoughts to analyse, to re-run events, to create imaginary scenarios, to pass comment, to critique, to worry and more. Most of our thoughts feel random.

But we can choose which to give our time and attention to. We can consciously choose to feed and nurture thoughts that lift our hearts. We can gently release those that don't; one thought at a time.

Start by noticing your thoughts. Catch yourself telling those stories. Do this with a light heart. It's not about 'getting rid' of any particular thoughts. It's about setting yourself free to choose which thoughts to encourage and nurture, and which to let gently flow past and away.

How about setting a reminder to stop and check what you are thinking at several points today?

If you don't set your intention, you are leaving your happiness to chance.

Setting our intention is like telling our unconscious mind which mental radio station to tune in to. If we set the intention to have a positive week, we will spot the things that go well and even challenging situations will feel more easily handled.

Imagine stubbing your toe as you get up in the morning: with no intention set, it's possible that this could set the tone for your day, with you continuing to notice everything that's going wrong – the classic 'woe is me' experience. But with a clear intention set that 'life is ok' or 'I choose to experience this moment', the stubbed toe remains a stubbed toe and doesn't ruin your day.

Without setting our intention, our experience of life is at the whim of our mind's mood.

Setting an intention for how you want to experience the day is a powerful way to create the life you are looking for.

Which intention do you choose to set today?

While you're telling yourself yesterday's story, you're missing out on today and tomorrow.

It's easy to get stuck in past dramas. And whilst those experiences can teach us valuable lessons, they don't have any right to dictate our future. Stories keep us stuck, justifying old behaviour and out-of-date beliefs. They keep us looking for more stories like them. We feed off the drama – it's an addiction.

While we're thinking yesterday's thoughts and telling yesterday's story, we're not moving on. We are giving all our power to the past. We are choosing – even if we're not consciously aware of it – to relive the old emotions and stresses from those stories. We miss the wonder of the 'here and now'. It stops us from creating wonderful new stories.

Just for today, how about spotting when you're telling a story? Pause and choose whether or not to continue to feed it.

There is nothing in our experience of life that we can't change.

We might not be able to change events or external circumstances, but we can change more about life than we might think. If something isn't working for us, we can either make changes to it or choose how we feel about it – and how we respond.

We might feel trapped – as though we're powerless victims – but that's not really true. We alone have power over our thoughts and feelings – and our actions, no matter what the scenario.

Our culture often teaches us the habit of thinking that our happiness is down to other people or things, but really it's an inside job. Right in this moment, we can change how we respond to what is going on in our life. The shifts we make today create our future.

And we have the power to make our present moment – and that future – the best and brightest they can be.

How about making today's choices really count?

Our biggest regrets are usually the things we didn't do; the chances we didn't take.

Although we might not be able to change the past, we can choose to stop living in regret – right now.

The past is done. We don't owe it our guilt and regrets. We can do our best to make good any harm done to others, but we can't go back and change what happened.

We have the power to choose – right in this moment – to seize life's wonderful experiences as they arise.

Is there something you want to do, but have been using your best excuses to avoid? How about zipping forward in time and asking the future 90-year-old you for some moral support and advice?

That 'future you' already knows which choices you wish you were making today. It wants to help you make sure you'll never again regret missed opportunities and will live life to the full.

Is it time to take the actions that your 'future you' will truly thank you for?

You don't need a floodlight to bring light to the darkness – a single flame will do.

How often do we hold back from doing what we feel drawn to do – at a deeper level – because we fear we aren't yet ready or are somehow inadequate?

We can put off living the life we are destined to live for a whole lifetime. But the world needs the light, laughter, healing and sunshine that you're here to bring – today.

Sometimes we set our expectations so high that we never get started. Or fear stops us from taking action. We are scared that we won't live up to our self-imposed standards. But how easily might that fear melt away, if we focus on lighting a single flame within us, rather than having to be responsible for the whole floodlight?

Your inner flame, even if it feels small to you right now, will inspire others to light their own candles and, before you know it, a floodlit stadium will appear.

Is it time to let your light shine today?

All criticism is borne of someone else's pain.

Native American Indian saying.

Happy people don't hurt others.

If someone lashes out and does or says something unkind to you, it's because they are hurting, deep down inside.

It doesn't make their actions or words ok. But it does help us shift our perspective from conflict to compassion, so we don't pick up their pain and carry it home in our hearts.

The next time someone has a go at you, how about pausing for a moment and acknowledging that pain, deep inside, which means they think that behaviour is ok?

When you respond from a place of compassionate understanding, you're not condoning their behaviour, but you are making sure you don't become its slave. And it could transform the outcome of the situation.

It's not about you. It never was. It's their 'stuff'.

Is there someone whose pain might benefit from your compassionate response?

No one can make you angry without your permission.

Yes, people can do their best to wind you up and 'press your buttons'. Some seem to have an Oscar-winning talent for giving us fuel to feel angry.

But no one can actually get inside your head and make the decision to feel angry for you.

No one can actually press the 'angry switch', without your consent.

How we feel – how we respond – is our choice; whether we like that or not.

Anger might be the easier option – your auto-pilot response – but that doesn't mean you have to go there.

It's always down to you.

And, of course, this doesn't just apply to anger. It's the same for happiness, sadness, stress, feeling inferior, feeling intimidated, worry, anxiety and any other emotion.

We always have the choice over which emotions to feed.

I'm curious: how might this help you today?

That which you can imagine, you can create.

Every man-made object started its life in someone's imagination, as an idea that inspired them.

Every organisation, every business, every charity, every course, every big event that has ever happened started off in someone's imagination.

If those people had given in to their fears and left the idea in their imagination, the world would have missed out on those experiences and gifts.

If you have an idea – a dream – that makes your heart sing, you owe it to yourself to allow it to come into your reality. Let your imagination feed it, let it grow, and then take inspired action.

Hand your fears and excuses over to the wisdom of your heart. Ask your inner wisdom to give you the courage you need.

By opening your heart and mind to possibilities, synchronicities and support, you can create that which you imagine.

What would you heart most like you to start creating today?

Do you know why you can't do it? It's in your 'because...'

"I can't do that, because…" holds the magic key to uncovering your excuses and limiting beliefs.

Our limiting beliefs and excuses are what hold us back from turning our dreams into reality and seizing the amazing opportunities that life throws our way – we even build them up into fears.

And once we know what they are, we can do something about them.

Simply being aware of those beliefs and excuses is the first step towards setting yourself free from them.

They're not real. You can't put them in a bag or hang them on a wall. They're just thoughts that have become habits.

And we can choose which thoughts to feed.

Want to shift some of those excuses and beliefs? Next time you catch yourself in a 'because' loop, ask yourself:

"Really?" … and watch what happens! You can choose whether to feed that 'because...' or to gently let it go.

If you cultivate the habit of saying kind things to yourself, you will transform your experience of life.

Our inner dialogue – often called the 'critic on your shoulder' – sets the tone for our experience of life.

If we're beating ourselves up and looking for what's wrong, then that is what we will also see in our outside world. And we'll attract more of it from the outside world, too, as though we were wearing a neon sign saying 'kick me'.

If we learn to treat ourselves with loving kindness and compassion, one thought at a time, just imagine how life will feel!

Let your inner voice choose a softer, kinder tone and you'll feel a near-instant sense of relief.

And you'll spot the evidence to support those loving thoughts in the world around you.

It doesn't matter what has gone before, you deserve to be treated with kindness – and that has to start within.

Which thought could you choose, right now, to be kind to yourself?

If you have a dream, the single most important thing you can do is to get started.

Without action, the dream will always remain just a dream – just an idea in your imagination.

But we're given our dreams for a reason. They're not intended to stay as ideas. They want to come to life.

Taking even the teeniest baby step to make a start will set things in motion.

No matter how scary it feels, your dream needs you to take that baby step, to bring it to life.

Thinking about a small step is much less daunting than heading towards the final outcome in one leap. And once you have taken that step, you can take another. And another.

Excuses melt away when we give ourselves a break from focussing on the end goal and split things down into more manageable chunks.

Take a tiny step towards your dream each day and, before you know it, you'll be there.

Which first step could you take today?

If what you're doing isn't working, do something different.

Forget the old saying, "If at first you don't succeed, try, try, try again."!

Doing the same thing, over and over, whilst expecting different results, simply doesn't make sense.

Doing what you have always done will keep you stuck where you always were.

Yes, keep going. But use all your senses and intuition to spot the tweaks that will take you to where you want to go.

It doesn't have to be about huge goals. It can be about any area of our experience of life.

Spinning round and round in the same gerbil wheel will never take you anywhere new.

Don't be afraid to make shifts in your approach, until you get to where you want to be.

Is there something about what you're doing that needs a tweak today?

I breathe all the way in. I breathe all the way out.

If your mind is racing, the most simple and effective technique to help you let go and cut your stress levels is Mindful Breathing.

How about trying it for a few moments, right now?

- Whatever you are doing, be still.

- Don't do anything to change or control your breathing; just accept it as it is.

- Then, as you breathe in (from just above your belly button, if that's comfortable for you), gently think, "I breathe all the way in."

- Breathe out whilst thinking, "I breathe all the way out."

- Keep going for a minute or two. If your mind wanders, gently bring it back to your breathing.

- That's it!

What did you notice?

How might life feel, if you were to practise this for one minute each hour, during stressful situations?

No amount of make-up, hairstyles or designer clothes will ever make you as beautiful as letting your inner radiance shine.

When did you last pay attention to nourishing your inner beauty? Most of us spend plenty of time covering it up – hiding it away. No matter how scary it might feel to let your inner beauty come out and play, your inner authentic self won't stop knocking at the door, until you do.

We feel it instantly when we meet someone whose inner beauty is shining. You can see it in their eyes and being around them lifts your spirits.

If you're up for truly shifting your experience of life, the good news is that it's simple and, unlike the latest anti-wrinkle cream, it's free. Every time you think a kind and loving thought, your inner glow increases. Every time you think a destructive thought, it decreases. It's that simple.

What could you do to remind yourself to nurture your inner radiance today?

Change hurts because of the stories we tell ourselves about it, not because the change itself is inherently painful.

Yes, some changes feel truly hard. But most – if we're honest – aren't that bad; we just build them up to feel that way. Tormenting and terrifying ourselves over change doesn't make us feel any better and stops us from making the shifts that we secretly yearn for.

To make a change feel easier, how about playing a quick game?

Imagine you have already made it and that you are now ten years in the future. Feel what you are feeling, ten years from now, having made that change. Think what you are thinking. Notice the kinds of things you say and do. Look back at the present you and thank them for having made the change.

Notice what advice that future you gives to the present you.

Now, coming back to the present moment, how much easier does that change feel now?

Don't believe everything your mind tells you.

Our mind is doing its best. In fact, it's doing exactly what we have trained it to do. It tells us stories. It passes comment. It evaluates. It tells us what to do and how to feel.

But it can only speak from the perspective of the filters, experiences, beliefs, hopes and fears it has picked up over the years. So its view is biased. **It's more of an illusion than a statement of fact.**

But we believe everything it tells us.

If it tells us we can't do something, we believe it. If it tells us that our dreams are unrealistic, we believe it. If it tells us that things will go wrong, we believe it.

Just because your mind tells you something is so, it doesn't mean it is.

It's ok to question what our mind tells us. It is full of opinion and prejudice; assumptions and leaped-to conclusions based on a lifetime of practice. And that's ok… if we also connect with the true wisdom of our hearts.

Do I really want to believe what I am telling myself today?

Life isn't meant to be taken as seriously as our thinking minds would have us believe.

In the Western culture, most of us have trained our minds to analyse, critique, evaluate, recount stories, worry, remember facts and spot problems. There's no problem with all of this, unless it squeezes out our natural ability to have fun, laugh, look for the positives and have a light heart.

Taking life too seriously is a Western addiction.

To turn things around, it's time to lovingly retrain your mind to enjoy life. You might need to practise giving yourself permission first, if you're not used to allowing yourself to have fun.

One of the easiest ways to do this is to spend ten minutes a day doing something that you really love – something that lifts your heart and brings a grin to your face.

Allow sunshine to wash through your day-to-day thoughts. Nurture thoughts that help you to feel good. It doesn't take long to shift that old pattern. Play with smiling more than you frown.

Is it time to think some sunshine thoughts?

We feel most like giving up just before we reach our goal. Keep going five minutes more!

Sometimes, even when we have tried hard and kept going, we give up on our goal at the final hurdle. Something goes wrong, we get demoralised and we throw in the towel.

We convince ourselves that we have had enough and we give up. We might post-rationalise the decision by telling ourselves that it wouldn't have worked out, anyway. Why do we do that?

It might be that we're scared of succeeding, so we sabotage our results. Or it could be that the timing wasn't yet right and other elements aren't yet in place. There are many reasons.

But don't give up. Believe in your dreams.

See them as already real. Feel them as already real. Daydream about how it feels, to live your life when they have already come into being.

Do this whenever you get a spare moment in your day and it will carry you through to your destination. It's inevitable.

Don't ever give up on your dreams.

If, as children, we were never taught the word 'should', our adult experience of life would be transformed.

'Should', 'I have to', 'I ought to' and their friends rob us of our freedom to choose.

We give these words our power and end up changing who we are and what we do, to match our perception of what is expected of us.

We fill our lives with a sense of obligation and guilt, to make sure we meet the requirements of all those 'shoulds'.

But none of this is real!

Yes, countries have laws to govern reasonable behaviour, but most of the 'shoulds' we run are in our minds. They're an illusion. At best, they're a guess. At worst, they're a life-limiting mistake. You don't have to let your 'shoulds' rule your world.

What's the answer?

"I choose to" is available to us in every moment and can radically shift your experience of life.

Doing what you know you need to do, even when you're not in the mood, is what will take you to the life of your dreams.

Having a dream is great. Taking those early steps is wonderful. But that doesn't get you to your goal.

It's consistent effort and dedication that gets you to where you are heading. It's especially important when life gets busy or challenges appear in our path.

Inspiration gives us the idea.

Motivation gets us started.

But it's the combination of **habit, routine and consistent action** that fuel our journey and create the change.

How could you remind yourself to nurture that habit today?

A good laugh and long sleep are the two best cures for anything.

Proverb

Ok, so they might not fix everything, but these two vital ingredients for a happy life can make a big difference.

Laughing releases endorphins – the body's natural feel-good chemicals – which will lift your mood, no matter what's going on.

It doesn't even matter if the laughter doesn't feel real at first. Your body's hormones will soon take over and produce the shifts you need to lift your mood.

Deep sleep allows the body to enter its self-healing state, while the mind processes and clears the day's experiences. This is why we wake up with solutions to problems we were stuck on, before we went to sleep. Good quality sleep is essential for a happy and healthy life.

When we're feeling down, we make every excuse as to why we can't laugh or sleep. But we can do it, if we choose to.

I'm curious: could a good laugh and a long sleep help you today?

The only way to change someone else's behaviour is to change your response.

How often do we catch ourselves wishing that the other person would behave differently?

"I wish he wouldn't say that!"

"I wish he wouldn't do that!"

The bad news is that we can't force the other person to change, any more than they could force us to change.

But it doesn't mean we have to put up with the situation.

We *can* change how we respond.

In the dance of any relationship, if we change our steps, the other person is likely to shift, too.

And even if they don't, we're likely to feel better about the situation, which is what's really important, isn't it?

Is there somewhere in your life today where a new response might set your free?

We believe the story we tell ourselves.

Beliefs aren't set in stone. And they change, over time. At some level, we choose them. But then we treat them as the ultimate Truth.

Out-of-date beliefs keep us stuck in the past, in old ways of thinking and behaving.

Our beliefs come from the stories we tell ourselves. If we tell ourselves we are a victim, then that's what we'll believe. If we tell ourselves that we are strong and confident, then that's what we'll believe.

Our unconscious mind sets its filters to collect evidence, from our day-to-day experience of life, to support those beliefs – to keep re-proving them. We'll filter out the evidence that contradicts them.

What can you do about all this?

You can choose whether or not you want to keep telling that old story, or whether you it's time for a new one. How about asking yourself:

"What might I have to believe, to tell myself this story? Is it really true? Is it a belief and story I want to keep telling, or is it time to let it go?"

Slowing down will help you get more done.

Rushing round on adrenalin, taking multi-tasking to near-Olympic levels, means we're living in a world where multi-tasking and moving fast are highly prized. We convince ourselves that there's never enough time.

But all the rushing comes at a price. It plunges us into the sympathetic nervous system's 'fight or flight' response, stressing our adrenals and using the part of the brain that is responsible for life-or-death short-term decision-making.

Multi-tasking means we're not really giving our awareness to any of the tasks we're doing, making it more likely that they won't be done properly. It also drags us into living through our thinking minds, rather than resting in the present moment and experiencing life through our physical senses.

Coming back to the present moment, being aware of your breathing, relaxing and releasing that stress response will allow you to slow down and – you can prove it to yourself – get more done by finishing one thing at a time.

What would happen if you slowed down a little today?

You see what you look for.

If you buy a red car, suddenly they're everywhere. Why is that? When we look for something, we tune the filters of our unconscious mind to notice it. To prevent us from feeling overwhelmed, our mind then filters out what we're not looking for.

But... That means if we're telling ourselves stories about what went wrong or the unkind thing that someone did, those filters get set to those frequencies and guess what you'll spot more evidence of? Yes, the experiences in your life that illustrate the core elements of those stories.

And you'll miss the proof of the things going well and people behaving kindly that surrounds us, every day.

Luckily changing those filters is as simple as choosing to feed the thoughts that lift your mood and lighten your heart.

If you spot yourself diving into a story that winds you up, ask yourself if that's what you really want. If not, let it go and choose to think thoughts that make you feel better.

Happiness is when what you think, what you say and what you do are in harmony.

Gandhi

Happiness is an inside job.

And it's entirely our choice.

Notice how Gandhi didn't say that happiness is when Fred does what we wanted or when Joe talks to us in the 'right' tone of voice. It's about us. We have the power within us to feel happy, through our choices – our thoughts; our words; our deeds.

If we think one thing, but say or do another, it creates an internal imbalance. At some level, part of us knows it doesn't feel right. It's not congruent. It creates an inner conflict. Yet it's a habit that many of us have in our society.

We do or say what we mind-read others want us to, then we wonder why we feel bad. Happiness can never be built on a foundation of pretence. It demands that we be true to who we really are.

Is there somewhere in your life that could do with a bit of realignment on this one today?

Being authentic to yourself is the key to feeling at peace in your world.

If we are pretending to be anything other than who we really are, it will never lead to inner peace. There will always be a conflict, deep down inside that niggles away at us.

Telling the truth to yourself has to be the starting point for figuring out who you really are – so you can be that person with those around you. If we pretend to be someone we're not, then our unconscious mind rightly reads this as criticism and rejection, leading to unhappiness.

Being your authentic, genuine self can feel scary. But how would you feel if you thought those around you couldn't be who they really are around you? So how might those around you feel if they realised you were hiding your true, beautiful self?

If you're not happy with who you feel you are, then it's ok to ask for help to make changes. They don't have to be big to have an impact.

Sometimes accepting yourself, just as you are, is the most important thing you could ever do.

Is it time to choose the path you wish to walk?

Too many a life is spent in walking the default path – the one our society chose for us, or the one our parents chose for us, or the one our teachers or even our peers chose for us.

It can feel easier to keep going on that path, rather than to stop and make a conscious choice about where you want to go.

In fact, we often don't know what we want.

It doesn't mean you're criticising or rejecting those who previously helped with your choices. It's ok to grow, to shift, to change, to realise that who you are now is no longer who you were then. And when that happens, sometimes the path needs to change.

We can always choose to change direction. If you're still breathing, then it's not too late.

Yes, it can feel scary, making those changes. But surely it's less scary than reaching your final breath and realising you never made them?

Is it time to choose another path? Who could you ask for support?

There's no point in heading towards a destination in life unless your heart is in the journey.

Life is too short to head somewhere for the sake of it.

Life is too short to keep on heading down a road that no longer feels right to you.

We are here to live with heart and soul.

If your heart isn't in the journey, then what's the point in heading to that destination?

If the experience isn't making your heart sing, then it's time to review where you're heading – and the way you're choosing to get there.

It doesn't mean you have to change track, but you might need to tweak your attitude to get back into alignment with your path.

You'll know if this is resonating for you today.

And your inner wisdom is waiting for you to connect with it, to give you the answers you are looking for on this one.

Does your heart have a message for you about your journey?

Whether you laugh your way through life or cry your way through, the destination is the same for all of us. So how about enjoying the journey?

It's easy to get so lost in 'self-help' books and courses that we become convinced that there's something 'wrong' with us that needs fixing – and that making changes in our lives is something that needs complicated tools and intricate belief systems.

Along the way, we pick up the belief that change has to hurt and has to be taken seriously.

But there's a simple – and free – change we could all make today that would transform our journey through life: **Laugh as you live**.

Think thoughts and take actions every day that lift your heart and bring a smile to your face. Laugh more than you frown; give thanks more than you complain and your experience of life will transform in just a few days.

Are you stuck on feeling angry?

It's funny how we are so good at getting angry, but trying to suppress it, because it's more socially acceptable to behave calmly and quietly.

I'm not advocating random rage around the place, but suppressing and denying strongly-felt emotions can cause us to shut down (even at a cellular level, which is now proven to lead to disease). The uncomfortable emotions shout louder, until they finally get our attention.

Yucky-feeling emotions are an early warning system to tell us when something isn't right; that we need to take action. Rejecting them and pretending they don't exist doesn't make us more 'spiritual' or 'emotionally mature'; it makes us more repressed and shut-down.

To deny strong emotions is to deny your intuition. And the more you deny your intuition, the less often you will hear it.

It's not the emotions that are the problem. It's the actions we take as a result of them... and we can always choose how to respond.

Is there an emotion screaming for your attention today?

Beliefs, like clothes, were never intended to be worn forever. If they're tired out and no longer fit, it's time to say goodbye!

Got any old beliefs hanging around in there, that no longer serve your highest good?

How about having a good rummage and clearing a few out?

Letting them go is much less effort than hanging on to them and looking after them, year after year, as they keep you stuck in old habits and out-dated ways of living.

And you get all the fun of choosing the new replacements, as an added bonus.

Letting go of them is simply a matter of choosing. "I choose to let go of this belief; I don't need it any more."

And then get curious: "What would my 'future me' like me to believe instead?"

That's it!

Which worn-out, old beliefs could you choose to let go of today?

You don't have to listen to the news.

Have you ever noticed how addicted we can get to the news, whether on the TV, the radio, the internet or in the newspaper?

But how often do we notice how it makes us feel? We consume it on auto-pilot, but does it uplift us? Or does it serve as a constant, drip-feeding soundtrack of how terrible things are, out in the 'real world'?

Most of us are addicted to drama. And bad-news-type-drama sells more papers and gets higher viewer ratings than good news.

What would happen if we were to become 'conscious consumers' of our news, choosing what to pay attention to, rather than just having it running in the background?

The world isn't going to stop turning if we put ourselves on a 'bad news diet' for a few days. And it won't mean we don't care about others. But it might give us space to remember how much sunshine is out there in our day-to-day lives.

Could you do with a bad news diet?

An excuse isn't real. It's just than a thought that you've had a bit more often than is helpful.

Neuroscientists have proven that a thought we think regularly becomes hard-wired in our brain, like a well-trodden footpath. It is easier and quicker for our mind to follow that path than a one that is newly-formed and still overgrown.

An excuse is a thought we have had often enough that it becomes a well-worn path and we no longer just think it, we believe it to be Truth. Once we believe it, it becomes a filter in our unconscious mind for our experience of life, controlling our auto-pilot behaviours and influencing whether we notice evidence that supports or contradicts it.

But it's not real. It's nothing more than a neural pathway, like any other thought.

And we can create new, more resourceful pathways by choosing to think and feed more empowering thoughts. Then the old excuses disappear.

Do you have any excuses that it's time to show the door to?

Are you wondering how to drop those old excuses?

Old excuses get in the way of us doing what we dream of doing, but we have given them the power of choice over our actions, to the point where they become deeply-held beliefs and even fears.

But they're nothing more than neurological pathways in our brain that can be changed, like any other thought habit.

Once the excuse becomes a belief, our unconscious mind will be pretty convinced of the Truth of it, so simply using affirmations to contradict it is more likely to set up an internal conflict than to produce positive results.

Instead of going into a head-on battle, you're better off selling your mind the idea that the old excuse is ready for an upgrade.

You want to open it up to the idea of possibilities – and 'wondering' with curiosity is a great way of doing that. Let your imagination do the hard work for you:

"I wonder if I could do it... I wonder what it might feel like, once I have done it..."

Have you ever noticed that birds never look backwards when they're flying?

So much of our time is spent dwelling on the past, telling 'Once upon a time stories'.

Yet if we're always looking in the rear view mirror, we can't see where we're going and aren't very likely to get there.

Of course, we can learn from the past.

But hanging around there steals your present and your future from you. And the present moment is where all of your choices are.

If you know where you're heading, then looking backwards doesn't really help.

So, if you're ready to spread your wings and fly, how about looking forwards and going for it today?

Do something today that your 'future you' will thank you for.

Who you are today is the product of all the 'yous' in the past – all their decisions; their choices; their thoughts; their actions.

Whether you like those decisions or not (ain't hindsight great!), you are who you are in this moment. Your future you doesn't want you to get stuck feeling negative about the past. The person you want to be in the future needs you to make changes in this present moment, to allow them to exist.

How about imagining having a chat with that 'future you'? Find a quiet moment. Take some relaxing deep sighing breaths and then imagine you are talking to the 'future you'. Hear what they have to say to you, without editing!

You'll find they're your greatest adviser and most vibrant cheerleader. They are the 'you' that has already made the changes, so they know what it felt like to go through it and are there to support and encourage you.

What could you choose to do, say or think today, that your 'future you' will thank you for?

Every expert was once a beginner.

If your heart is calling you to do something, to learn a new skill, to start a new hobby or even to change your career, give yourself a break and allow yourself to start as a beginner.

They moved from beginner to virtuoso by learning from their mistakes and by keeping going with consistent practice, even when they weren't in the mood.

It's easy to forget that each and every skill we currently have started from a zero point.

How about letting go of judging the speed or quality of your progress?

Embrace the excitement and fun of learning and growing. Become a fan of curiosity, as you travel through the experience.

It's ok, whatever progress you make. It all takes time and practice. And you might as well enjoy the journey.

Above all, make a start – even just a teeny start – perhaps today?

When you deal with the need that the old habit was meeting, change becomes easy.

One of the problems with making changes is that old habits are satisfying some unmet need, even if we're not consciously aware of it. It's called 'secondary gain'.

If you try to change without addressing that secondary gain, it will be hard work, taking masses of willpower, and your unconscious mind will still be looking for ways to meet that need – probably with a new habit.

To find out what the secondary gain is that has been keeping you stuck, so you can find more healthy ways of meeting or releasing that need, you can ask yourself: "How has that old habit been serving me? Which need is it meeting?"

And if you need to go deeper, send your head into a spin, bypassing your mind's rational filters, getting to the root of the matter with: "What *won't* happen if I *don't* make the change?"

Uncover the unmet need, deal with it compassionately, and change becomes easy.

All the beauty in the universe can be found in a single raindrop.

The smallest and most simple things in life are filled with beauty, as much as the most dramatic landscape.

And the beauty and perfection of the raindrop; the majesty of the mountain range; are created by the same energy as every cell in your body.

Every part of you is a magnificent creation, even the more wobbly bits you might want to hide away from view!

Opening your heart to learning to love yourself, just as you are, is the most profoundly life-changing thing you could ever do.

What could you choose to think, right now, to make a start today?

Nothing changes without action.

Leave things as they are and that's how they'll stay.

Sounds obvious? But it's amazing how often we expect things to shift, without taking action or doing anything about it.

The action might be as quiet as choosing to feed different thoughts. Or it might be as big as moving country.

Whatever it is, action produces change. Ideas, on their own, don't.

How different might life feel, if we saw it as a journey where we could create opportunities to make the shifts we want, rather than waiting for external circumstances to change for us?

You are the architect of your dreams. But even the most beautifully-designed house remains as a picture on paper until someone takes action to build it.

Is there somewhere in your life calling you to take action today?

Your dreams will only be as big as your excuses allow.

Our excuses – also known as limiting beliefs – are what stop us from making shifts in life and hold us back from what we want to achieve.

Our excuses directly limit the scale to which we take action on our dreams.

The first step to doing something about your excuses is to spot them. Fortunately it's easy – simply complete this sentence with your gut response: "I can't be / do that, because…"

Once you've found the excuse, you're free to choose whether or not you want to keep feeding it, or perhaps things have moved on and it's out of date. There's nothing wrong with those old excuses. You don't need to beat yourself up over them. But you don't need to hang on to them, either. It's ok to release them.

To let excuses go, you can visualise them gently melting away. Or you could break your dream into smaller steps, so the excuse loses its power.

As soon as you stop telling yourself the stories that justify those old excuses, you'll find they shrink and fade of their own accord.

Kindness is in our power, even when fondness is not.

Samuel Johnson

Behaving kindly towards someone who has behaved badly towards you can feel challenging.

It doesn't mean you are pretending to like them.

It doesn't mean that their behaviour was acceptable.

It means you are choosing to connect, with compassion, with the essence of that person, who must be feeling pain, to behave badly.

None of us is perfect. We all lash out at times, even towards ourselves.

Learning to respond with kindness, even when friendship is beyond our power, sets us free from the cycle of pain that would otherwise be created.

It can feel tough, but it instantly diffuses conflict, both in your external world and in your heart. And it means that their behaviour won't ruin your day.

Is there somewhere in your life where kindness might be in your power today?

You can repeat that old auto-pilot response again. Or you could take a deep breath, pause and reclaim your choice.

A scary amount of our behaviour is running on auto-pilot – quick-fire responses and behaviours triggered by the re-running of old memories.

Some, like taking action to avoid an accident, are useful. Others, like responding emotionally to someone's behaviour, can be destructive.

They are based on 'old programming' from past experiences and can get out of date.

It keeps us stuck in old behaviours and habits, long after they have finished serving any useful purpose.

Fortunately, becoming aware of those old auto-pilot responses is all that's needed to give us back our choice. Taking a deep breath and relaxing can give you a moment to consider how you really want to respond this time.

Do I really want to respond that way this time? Or would I like to choose another path?

Your excuses will disappear, as soon as you stop defending them.

Our excuses only have power over us because we give them that power.

We defend them; we justify them; we collect evidence to support them; we tell people about them; we tell ourselves about them; we let them choose what we can or can't do or become.

But as soon as you let go of sticking up for those old excuses, as soon as you open your heart to the possibility that they're not 100% true, you'll realise that they never really had the right to limit your experience of life.

They're not 'real'.

When you set yourself free from their grip, you open up the possibility of living life to your full potential. You reclaim your power to choose who to be; how to experience life; what to do; which future to create.

Life is too short to allow our excuses to make so many important choices for us.

Is it time to reclaim your power and stop defending your excuses?

How different might life feel if you realised that your story is just a story?

Our thinking mind has been trained to tell us stories. It analyses; it embellishes; it adds drama and commentary.

But our unconscious mind – the bit that's running the show – acts on those stories as though they are real.

It triggers the same chemical reactions in your body that produce the same stresses and emotions as it would if you were actually experiencing those events, live.

And all of this sets the tone for our inner dialogue, filters our experience of life and impacts our actions.

Once we know all this, surely it's time to choose those stories with a little more care? It's not about 'getting rid' of them.

But we do have the power to choose which stories to feed and which to lovingly, firmly release..

What might shift if you were to let go of some of those old stories today?

Imagining a change is almost as good as doing it.

Athletes visualise performance improvements, before they make them. Performers mentally rehearse. Running through a presentation in your mind helps the 'real event' run more smoothly. Your unconscious mind reacts the same way, whether what you are thinking about is happening now, or is just in your imagination.

Imagine the change you want to make. Now take a step into the future, to the time after you have made that change. Notice how your posture is, having made that change. Become aware of the thoughts you are thinking, with that change behind you. See the things you do and say, having been through that change. Feel the post-change emotions – right now.

While you are doing this, you are creating new neurological pathways in your brain, to support that change. You are laying the foundations for the new behaviour, before you have even had to do anything, giving you a head start. Do this every day and the shifts you're dreaming of become inevitable!

Doesn't that make the change feel easier?

No matter what is going on or how you are feeling, you can turn things around by finding something to say 'thank you' for.

Sometimes life can feel tough. We can get lost in the challenges we are facing, dragging us down.

But no matter what is going on, if we want to turn things around, we can shift our experience by finding things we are grateful for. Spending even just a minute saying thank you for things you appreciate in life shift your thoughts, feelings and actions.

And it's a wonderful way to start and finish your day. Take a quiet moment and say a heartfelt 'thank you' for at least ten things in your life – even things as fundamental as breathing or still being alive. Keep going for at least 60 seconds.

It is a deceptively simple yet profoundly powerful technique.

Want help? For daily inspirational gratitude emails visit: www.MiracleOfGratitude.com

Imagine how saying thank you could help, when times are tough.

It's impossible to feel happy while you're thinking miserable thoughts.

At the most basic level, our emotions are chemical reactions in our bodies that last around a minute. These processes are triggered by our thoughts.

A sad feeling is triggered by 'feeding' a sad thought. A happy feeling is triggered by feeding a happy thought. And these chemical reactions last for about a minute. The only way an emotion can last for longer than its natural minute is if our thoughts keep feeding it and re-triggering that chemical reaction.

If you're feeling down, it means that relief is only ever a thought away. Think a more uplifting thought and you'll be shifting those chemical reactions and also your emotions.

Whichever topic you choose, you are taking a positive step to influence those chemical reactions, helping you to feel better. How about asking yourself:

"What could I choose to think about right now that could help me to feel a little better?"

Inspiration without action will never lead to anything more than a 'nice idea'.

The action doesn't have to be huge. It might be as simple as starting to talk about what is inspiring you.

Though new-age texts tell us we can 'think things into reality', it's easy to forget that we live in a world where it's our actions, based on those thoughts, that create what we most want to see.

Something magical starts to happen when you take action on your inspiration; on the ideas that make your heart sing.

It's as though you're saying "Yes!" to the universe and its entire synchronicity toolkit.

And if you take a tiny action each day, before you know it, what inspired you will be part of your day-to-day reality.

What is inspiring you – calling to you – today? And what action will you take?

Are you sowing seeds of worry or hope?

Each time you worry, it's as though you are sowing, watering and nurturing seeds of worry, until they become strong and vibrant worry-plants.

The same goes for any type of thought.

The seeds we sow we later reap through our experience of life.

What's the answer?

We can choose which seeds to water.

No one can force you to water 'worry seeds'.

If you don't like the way a thought makes you feel, then you probably don't want it to grow into a full-sized tree. So don't water it.

Gently release it – let it go – and move on to the next one.

How about becoming a conscious chooser of which thoughts you want to sow and nurture?

The answers you are seeking aren't 'out there'; they're waiting patiently inside you.

All the wisdom you'll ever need is already there inside you. All you need to do is calm your mind for long enough to hear it.

Take a deep breath and breathe out with a relaxing sigh, gently letting go of your need to keep asking. Repeat a few times until you feel yourself relax. Now set your intention to listen to your inner wisdom.

Even if you don't get an answer immediately, it will come.

Look for the signs – it might be in the words of a song, or a picture on a billboard, or a comment from a stranger. You'll know when it's your inner wisdom, rather than your thinking mind, because the answer will resonate for you – and it will always be wise and kind.

If you need help quietening your mind, check out www.DailySunshine.co.uk/bonus

Practise this daily and you'll find it becomes easy to let your inner guidance become a central part of your life.

Keeping a notebook of happiness quick fixes could change your life.

We can change how we feel by changing what we're thinking or doing. And it takes just 60 seconds to shift the chemical reaction in your body that produce your experience of emotions.

When we're stuck feeling bad, it can be hard to remember the quick fixes that lift our mood. The grumpy story can easily take over and sabotage our efforts to feel better.

So how about keeping a list in your bag or wallet of 'quick fixes' that help you turn things around, no matter how you're feeling?

They're different for each of us. Going back to a happy memory works well. You could use a photo as a visual reminder. Anything to do with physical movement works well, too, as does singing – even if it's not in tune!

Experiment with these fixes when you're feeling ok and it will be easier to remember to use them in tougher times – it will become second nature.

Use a happiness quick fix each day and it will transform your experience of life.

Comparing yourself to others only serves to demotivate you.

How often do we fall into the 'comparing' trap?

It starts at school (or younger) and by adulthood, we've nearly perfected the art.

It encourages us to wallow in the world of "I'm not good enough," and "I'll never do that as well as them."

Whatever it is that you are here to do, whatever makes your heart sing, you are the only person in the world who can do it. You have a unique combination of skills and experiences that nobody else can match.

How about, instead of comparing ourselves to others, we compare ourselves to our truly authentic inner selves? How about we set goals to help us move closer and closer towards thinking, feeling and acting from that place of inner Truth, rather than continuing to live life through the lens of an actor, playing a part?

"How 'me' am I being today?"

What could you do today, to move one step closer to allowing that inner beauty to become your outward reality?

Kindness, like a boomerang, always comes back.

This doesn't mean that we should expect the other person to do something for us in return. It's about how kindness impacts us, inside.

It helps us to feel good. If we're actively looking for ways to do kind deeds and to speak with compassion, we'll notice more kindness and compassion in the world around us.

It's not about 'agenda-based kindness', where we are kind because we want something. It's about 'non-attachment kindness', where we set the kind words and actions free to work their magic, without us needing to know what happened next.

If we train ourselves to focus on kindness, our inner dialogue – the way we talk to ourselves – will become more kind and less critical. This makes it easier for us to feel good about ourselves, which has a knock-on effect for all our thoughts and actions, as well as how far we go towards achieving our dreams. These are just some of the ways that our kindness can return to us.

Are you ready to create a happiness boomerang today?

It only takes a moment to break an old habit.

Forget the urban myth about it taking 21 days (or more!) to break a habit. The truth is that it is nearly instant – it happens as soon as you have made the decision to let that old habit go. That decision is a commitment to releasing the old habit and nurturing new, more empowering behaviours. What takes the time is remembering that you don't have that old habit any more. The effort comes with gently reminding yourself that you now have more choices.

But, once you have made that initial decision, it's easier than you might think. Without that clear decision, even the greatest amount of willpower won't give you the results you want. If you haven't bought into the decision 100%, you'll sabotage your results.

An easy way to help you crank up your commitment is to imagine how life might be in ten years' time, if you don't make the change. If that's not what you want, fill your home with sticky note reminders; set alarms on your phone; whatever it takes to support your decision.

What could you do today, to show your commitment to your decision?

Change can't happen until the pain of changing becomes less than the pain of staying the same.

Or, as Anasis Nin beautifully puts it:

"And the day came when the risk to remain a bud was more painful than the risk it took to blossom."

Being scared of making a change is ok. It simply means that it's outside of your current comfort zone. But we stretch and grow our comfort zones all the time – so you can do it again, if you want to.

At some deep level, you know how.

Breaking the change down into baby steps makes the shift easier and less scary.

How about allowing yourself to blossom, one petal at a time?

The sunshine in your heart is brighter than the one in the sky. All you need to do is let it shine.

It's amazing how much easier it can feel to do, say and think happy things, when it's sunny outside. How often do we forget, though, that's there's sunshine in our hearts, whenever we need it? It glows in a way the sun in the sky could never manage. That inner radiance is contagious. Spend time with someone with a sunny, light-hearted vibe and it lifts your mood.

Old hurts and fears, as well as cultural conditioning, mean we get into the habit of hiding that light. And we get into the routine of looking for happiness outside of ourselves.

The easiest way to reconnect with your inner sunshine is to become an ambassador for helping others to reconnect with theirs. As you spot ways of helping others to do this, your unconscious mind will automatically do it for you, too.

What could you do, think or say today, to help others (or yourself!) reconnect with that inner sunshine?

There's no point in making a decision, unless you're going to act on it.

Making a decision is not enough. Taking action, based on that decision, is what creates shifts in your life.

Making the commitment to take action – even just a baby step – is the magic key; the vital ingredient.

You could say that there's no point in making a decision, unless you're going to see it through.

If we make a decision, but don't act on it, it has a tendency to nag us – to keep reminding us that it's there. It can lead to us behaving in ways that aren't congruent with our true, authentic selves. It can create inner conflict, which leads to us feeling bad – and even behaving badly, whilst feeling guilty.

If you don't want to implement a decision, you really are better not making it at all. And that's ok.

If your heart's not in it, it might be better to leave that decision alone.

Are there any decisions that could do with some action today?

Perhaps the most important thing you can have when times are tough is hope.

It's easy to get lost in our stories of woe and worry. We convince ourselves that things will go wrong or get worse.

But if we allow little seeds of hope to grow in our hearts, we open up to the possibilities of things going well and improving; and this even becomes more likely. Those seeds of hope help us to spot the opportunities and synchronicities that can turn things around. If we were wearing our 'woe is me' glasses, we would be likely to miss them.

Is there a situation that's been stressing you, right now? How about spending a moment connecting with how you feel about it. If the emotions are too strong, imagine looking at yourself in a mirror, with that person feeling the emotions, instead of you.

Now allow a gentle wave of hope to start in your heart. Let it gently expand and grow until it washes through those emotions.

Notice how subtle, yet good, that shift feels?

Before seeing results, a gardener must first choose what to grow.

How often do we actually take the time to choose what we want to grow, to cultivate, to nurture or to create in our lives?

I'm talking about dreams, visions, personal characteristics and skills – even beliefs.

Scattering random seeds on the soil will produce plants, but they might not be the ones you want.

And it's ok to choose. Choosing doesn't mean we're judging or rejecting the seeds we choose not to sow. It simply means we are exercising discernment and taking positive steps to move towards wherever it is we next want to be.

If you were to make conscious choices about what to grow and nurture in your life today, what would you choose?
And are there any seedlings that might need some weeding?

'Who we are' has nothing to do with what we do or what we have.

So much of our identity – our sense of self and 'who we are' – is mistakenly built around what others think of us, what we do and what we own.

And it's illustrated by the fact that one of the most common first questions to ask a new acquaintance is "What do you do?"

But there's a world of difference between 'doing' and 'being'.

'What you do' is not who you are. You – the essence of your true self – is separate from your actions, habits, thoughts and behaviours. Yet our behaviour is often a tool we use to mask who we really are, as though we're scared of living authentically and being true to our inner radiance.

Who are you? Who do you really want to be? Which old fears, habits and beliefs could you lovingly release, today, to let that 'real you' come out to play?

You won't find out who you really are by looking at others.

It's funny how often we compare ourselves to others. But it usually leads to unhappiness. All we can ever see is our version of the illusion of reality, filtered through our mind's beliefs, fears, experiences and expectations. It's not real.

We might end up feeling superior, deciding that the other person isn't as good as us – not exactly a great basis for a relationship. Or we could feel inferior – and we all know what that does for our confidence and self-esteem.

If we're lucky, the comparison might serve as motivation for us to make changes. But our inner critic thrives on judging others and ourselves, so those changes are tougher than they need to be. You are who you are. They are who they are. Accepting and loving yourself for who you really are is the path to inner peace and happiness. You are already amazing. So why bother comparing that with others?

How about spending 60 seconds thanking yourself for all that you are, right now?

There is no space for gossip, when you fill your words with kindness.

Spreading gossip can feel like fun – entire magazine and news channels depend on our addiction to gossiping. And we are addicted to cranking up the drama in the story, to make it even more juicy and judgemental. But it's only gossip if there's someone to gossip about. And we all know from experience that being on the receiving end of idle rumours hurts.

Is that really what you want? Is hurting others for our own entertainment really how we want to live?

If you'd like to kick the habit, you might like to apply a simple question, before you speak. Ask yourself, "Would a compassionate person say this to their face?" If not, don't say it at all.

Before you share news, check whether your motivation is kindness. If not, how about not sharing it? I know it can be scary to break the habit, especially if we hang around with people who love to gossip. But surely it's worth it?

What steps could you take to fill your words with kindness today?

You'll never change your future if you keep thinking yesterday's thoughts.

Our thoughts are the triggers for our actions and emotions. They dictate what we pay attention to and influence which opportunities we grab, as well as those we allow to pass us by or even sabotage.

If we keep thinking the same things, we'll keep getting the same results.

Magically, turning things around is simple. How about asking yourself:

"Is this thought taking me closer towards or further away from where I want to be?"

If it's closer towards, then how about nurturing that thought – or an even better one?

If it's moving you away from your dream, gently let that thought pass and consciously choose another that helps you move back towards your destination. It takes practice, but all of us can do it – if we want to.

Are there any of yesterday's thoughts that you could let go of today?

What might the other person be thinking or feeling, right now, for them to believe that this behaviour is an appropriate choice?

Rather than rushing to judge or retaliate when someone behaves badly, how about asking yourself that question?

If you could put yourself in their shoes for a moment, what might be going on inside them, for them to behave that way?

Obviously, I'm not asking you to mind-read.

But taking a moment to see the world from their possible point of view, before jumping to conclusions and reacting in a way you might regret, could have a wonderful impact on both of your lives.

They are human – just like you. They have 'baggage' and fears – just like you.

How about treating them with the compassion that you both deserve – and watching the magic happen?

Are you listening to hear? Or listening to reply?

When you have a conversation with someone, is your inner dialogue talking to you about what the other person is saying? Or is it telling you what to say back?

It's amazing how easy it is to fall into the habit of 'listening to reply'.

And yet, not feeling heard is a painful experience in any relationship. Not feeling heard can push our buttons and provoke all kinds of behaviour that we'd rather avoid – from yelling and sulking to lashing out or shutting down. It undermines trust, prevents real communication and damages relationships.

Fortunately, there's a simple technique you can use to become someone who listens to hear:

Bring your awareness back to the present moment, focussing on the other person, by making eye contact. If your mind needs to chatter, how about telling it to repeat the intention, "I hear you."?

Is there someone in your life who really needs you to hear them today?

Life goes past too quickly to waste a single moment in regret.

Instead of telling ourselves stories that keep us stuck in sadness, regret, hurt, anger, resentment, guilt or bitterness, how about setting ourselves free to enjoy this moment – and the next one? And the next one?

How about asking yourself the question:

"Do I really want to give this moment to that old story or emotion? How could I choose to feel / what could I choose to think, right now, instead?"

Getting stuck in old 'stuff' – and wallowing in guilt and regret – changes nothing for the better. Any action or decision made from a place of guilt is likely to produce more guilt.

If you're feeling regret, how about using it as a trigger to change what you're doing in this moment, to create a more positive future? Then let it go – it has done its job.

It takes practice, but it will create the future you've been hoping for.

How about getting started today?

You – and only you – have the power to make changes in your life.

Sure, others can offer moral support, suggesting 'how' and playing the cheerleader role. But change comes from within. No one can do it for you. If we hang around waiting for someone else – or some book or some course or some guru – to manifest the changes for us, we'll have a very long wait. Hanging around, searching for the 'perfect technique', the 'right' workshop or 'the' book to do it for you is effectively delegating your personal power and free will to something outside of you, beyond your control.

The choices – the actions – that are needed to create shifts in our experience of life are ours, not anyone else's. And this is great news – because no one knows how you tick and what works for you better than you do! So the next time you catch yourself looking for someone or something to do the whole 'change thing' for you, how about remembering that you hold all the answers you need within yourself already?

What would your deepest wisdom suggest for you today?

Never underestimate the impact that a simple action might have in someone else's life.

Remember the times when a kind word or a thoughtful deed has made a difference for you? A smile from a stranger; an unexpected gift; someone giving way in busy traffic?

We can never know what's going on in someone else's world. But simple acts of kindness and helpful support can be the trigger for shifting someone's thoughts and mood, with an amazing ripple effect.

And being kind is free!

A supportive word for a colleague; eye contact and your undivided attention for a loved one; a helping hand for a person carrying a heavy bag up the escalator; these are acts that cost us nothing, other than a little bit of time.

And if we feel we're too busy to be kind, then perhaps we need to re-evaluate our priorities?

Whose life could you impact today?

In every experience we can choose to look for the sunshine or to see only the clouds.

We might not be able to choose all the events in our life, but we can choose how to experience them.

In every moment, we can choose whether to focus our attention on the stuff that upsets us; the drama, the worry and the things that are going wrong. Or we can give more of our 'thought time' to what is ok and what might go well.

We're not denying the 'bad bits'; we're simply choosing what to spend our timing focusing on.

Changing the way we see things makes the things we see change. Shifting the balance of what you are focussing on is one of the fastest ways to change your life. And all you need to do is practise – one thought at a time. If you forget, that's fine. Just pick it up again when you remember.

Is there something in your life today where looking at it differently could change things?

If you really want to make that change, you'll find a way. If you don't, you'll find an excuse.

If we're not really committed to making a change, every excuse and every way we have of procrastinating will get in the way.

We will sabotage even our most valiant efforts, often just moments before success.

The more you want to make that shift, the more easily those old limiting beliefs and excuses will move out of the way; the more easily you'll find the time and motivation to keep going; the more likely you are to achieve your aim.

And if you don't really want to make the change, then why bother?!

Do you really want to make that change today? Or is it time to let it go and move on?

If you believe you can't change, then you won't.

If, deep down, you truly believe that a change is not possible, then that is what you will experience.

Your unconscious mind will set its filters to spot only the events that support that belief, ignoring any evidence to the contrary. It's brilliant at it!

It will draw your attention to experiences, messages and events that prove you are right.

And the more strongly you believe it isn't possible, the more likely you are to sabotage your best efforts, rather than allowing yourself to experience the success that would violate your mind's core beliefs of what is true.

The great news is that being aware of those beliefs – catching yourself thinking about them – is often enough to start the process of shifting them.

You might like to ask yourself the question:

Is there anything I believe about my likelihood of success in this venture that could be jeopardising my chances?

You don't have to believe you can. You just need to believe that it might be possible.

There's no point in trying to steam-roller over old beliefs, to prove them wrong. Your mind has been diligently collecting evidence for years, to support and prove the truth of that belief.

If a researcher tells people that a long-believed theory is wrong, their news is often rejected and ridiculed, before it is accepted. Our mind works the same way.

Rather than denying that old belief, soften it. Open your mind to the possibility that something else might be true. This creates new choices. It reduces your mind's resistance, melts away fear, prevents inner conflict and makes it less likely that you'll sabotage your success.

It allows new thoughts to bubble up and be nurtured, which can lead to new behaviours and eventually new, healthier habits. When you let all of this happen, the old beliefs about what you could or couldn't do are no longer relevant – they melt away.

Which change might you choose to believe could be possible today?

Our thoughts choose our words and actions for us.

When we think angry or unkind thoughts, we end up saying or doing angry and unkind things.

If we get into the habit of gently releasing thoughts that make us feel bad and nurturing thoughts that make us feel good, it will filter through to the way we talk to ourselves, the way we talk to others and the things we do.

But most of us think our thoughts are beyond our control. They feel like a random assortment of ideas over which we have no influence.

Fortunately that's not the case.

Though philosophers and sages may debate where thoughts originate from, once one is there, we can choose whether or not to play with it. If we don't like it, we can accept it, stop feeding it and let it naturally drift away and then move on to the next one.

If you practise letting go of thoughts that make you feel bad and feeding thoughts that make you feel good, then over time, it will become your habitual way of interacting with the world.

How might this help you today?

117

A loving atmosphere in your heart is the foundation for a happy and loving life.

If we spend our time beating ourselves up, our heart becomes filled with fear, judgement and criticism. Most of us have practised this for decades. But if you put effort into nurturing compassion towards yourself, you allow flowers of hope and happiness to grow in your heart.

One thought at a time, we can ask ourselves whether we are being kind to ourselves or causing pain; whether it is moving us towards a happy heart or away from it. Our self-criticism isn't based on Truth. It generalises events: "I *always* get that wrong." "It *never* works out." If you catch yourself at this, you can ask the simple question: "Really? Who says?" and perhaps "What could I say to myself that's more loving?"

Eventually, once we have played with this enough, it becomes a wonderful habit. The way we treat ourselves has a profound impact on every aspect of our life and relationships.

Is there something you could do today to help foster a loving atmosphere in your heart?

Happiness is our natural state. Everything else is a learned habit.

Watch babies or young children and you'll see that after a tantrum or setback their natural equilibrium state is 'happy ok-ness'.

They don't spend days telling themselves stories about how terrible it was or re-living those painful emotions.

Unlike us, they haven't developed the habit of staying stuck in yucky-feeling emotions.

The only thing that keeps us from returning to our happy equilibrium is habit – replaying the situation in your mind; going through 'what if…?" scenarios.

But habits can change.

The next time you spot yourself doing the 'tell-story-feel-bad' thing, how about asking yourself the question:

Do I really want to go there? No? What would I like to think instead?

It really is that simple. It only gets more difficult if you tell yourself it will be.

If someone gives you feedback, try it on for size, before you believe it.

People can be somewhat free and generous with their opinions – even when it comes to giving others feedback about their performance, behaviour, beliefs, values or lifestyle.

When we're on the receiving end of that feedback, it's easy for it to bypass our brain's rational filters, finding its way straight to the 'this is true' part of our mind – especially if we respect or fear the other person or their opinion agrees with that of our inner critic.

If someone tells us something negative, we can take it on board; believe it and – worst of all – let it cloud our future actions and decisions.

But here's a solution: treat the feedback like a woolly jumper.

Try it on for size. If it fits, accept it and choose whether you want to do anything about it. If it doesn't fit, gently let it go and move on. It has no place in your life.

The people who bug you are often your biggest mirrors.

There can be a hidden gift in the behaviour of those who bug us the most. If you find that several people are annoying you with the same behaviour, then chances are that it's time to look in the mirror.

If you were to write down a list of the top 3 behaviours that currently irritate you in others, then it's likely this is because you don't want to admit that you're prone to them, too. It's easiest to criticise in others that which we least want to accept in ourselves.

It takes a huge dollop of honesty to become aware of and to accept behaviours that we were denying. But this sets us free to do something about them – and to stop wasting energy covering them up. But that's how we set ourselves free from those out-of-date habits. So, in a weird way, the person bugging you could be offering you a great gift.

Are you ready to take a look in the mirror and set yourself free today? Amazing things are waiting for you on the other side.

Watch out who you're letting rent the space in your head. It's ok to evict any tenant who's dragging you down.

It's easy to spot someone who's squatting in your head space. You spend much of your time thinking and talking about them – complaining about their behaviour and telling everyone how unkind / angry / mean they are. It's a classic 'woe is me' experience, because we're giving all of our personal power to that other person. We are letting their behaviour have a massive impact on our experience of life.

We feel irritated and stressed about the situation and our mind's story machine goes into over-drive. It impacts other areas of your life and the way you are feeling, throughout your day.

How can you evict them? It's not about rejecting or avoiding them. As usual, it's an inside job. Stop telling yourself the story. Be brutally honest with yourself, looking for the Truth in the situation; stick to the objective facts; letting go of the drama.

Is there someone who needs evicting today?

Is it time to set yourself free from the drama?

Here's a simple 3-step action plan to set you free from the drama of the stories your mind might be telling you – to let you move on and feel happier.

1. Ask yourself (very honestly) "What's the Truth in this? And what's drama and embellishment?" Let go of everything that's drama. Feel it dropping away. Cut those invisible ties. It might be hard, but you'll feel better – instantly – especially if you do this with compassion for yourself and the others involved, rather than anger and rejection.

2. Ask yourself: "Do I need to take any specific action to improve the situation?" If yes, do it. If no, move on. Remember, the action might be as simple (yet powerful) as you shifting your attitude towards the situation.

3. Each time the drama pops back up, remind it that you're no longer playing that game. Don't feed it. Just let it pass. Choose to think of something that brings you relief.

How might letting go of the drama help you today?

There's a difference between the action and the actor.

Sometimes people do stuff that's not acceptable.

It's easy to hold resentments or to want to retaliate in some way. We can direct our painful emotions towards them and can even stay awake, half the night, replaying the movie of how unkind and unfair their actions were.

But there's a difference between the person and their actions. The actions – their behaviour – are the outward appearance of the person. What is deep down inside, the essence of that person, is not the same. At some level, they are running the same kinds of auto-pilot responses that we do. At some level, they want to be happy and feel at peace – just like us, even if it doesn't look like it on the outside.

Like actors in a play, what we show the outside world isn't necessarily the Truth of who we really are, but a script that we have rehearsed well. When we remember that, we set ourselves free to choose a response for the highest long-term good, rather than short-term retaliation.

Are you ready to create a space between their action and your response, to reclaim your choice?

Want to feel as free as a Friday, every day of the week?

We all know that 'Friday feeling' – when we finally get to hop off the week's treadmill and feel free to make our own choices, all weekend. Can you imagine what it would feel like to feel completely free, every day?

Whatever 'freedom' means to you, it's something that we are striving for, yet find so hard to capture. But there's a secret: **freedom is an inside job**. It isn't something anyone can 'give you' or 'take away'.

Yes, we might feel we're not free – and we might not be able to easily change our current environment – but we can always choose our experience of our situation. And that's true freedom.

You are free to choose your thoughts. You are free to choose your emotions. You are free to choose your actions. All of this freedom – and more – is yours already.

How would it be if you were to choose a mantra along the lines of "I feel free today"?

So how about creating a freedom experience for yourself today?

Forgiveness, letting go of the past, is the only way you'll ever set your future free.

While we stay stuck in the past, clinging to the old hurts and resentments, it is impossible to move towards a happier future. Those old wounds can give us a sense of identity or self-justification, but we will never be free to live our present or future to the full. **It's impossible to live happily in the present moment while you're holding on to the past.**

It doesn't mean you have to pretend that old hurts were ok or condone the behaviour. But imagine how that person was feeling, to be able to behave in that way; happy people don't hurt others. Perhaps you could find it in your heart to feel compassion for their inner pain?

But if you can find it in your heart to forgive the soul-level of the person behind the behaviour, and then cut your ties with the old story, you will experience profound shifts in your life that open your heart to feeling pace and joy again.

Surely your future is worth letting go of old wounds? Isn't it time to let them heal?

If everything were possible, how big would you dream?

Our hearts only give us dreams that, at some level, are possible. With enough courage, hope, belief and action, all barriers and obstacles can be overcome.

A dream – a vision – that gets you excited, one that makes you want to take action, comes with everything you need to walk its path, no matter what your fears or old excuses might tell you.

Yes, it might feel scary; you might need to ask others for help. Yes, there might be new skills to learn and support to seek out. But it's possible.

If it really resonates for you; if it really nags you and keeps coming back to you, then you can find a way to make it happen. All you need to do is to open up to believing that it is possible. In fact, your dreams aren't just possible – they're already waiting for you.

How about connecting with that 'future you' who is already living that dream and living your life, today, from their viewpoint?

How big could you choose to dream today?
Your dreams are waiting for you!

Do something every day that inspires you and watch the miracles queue up for you.

When we consciously choose to think thoughts and to take actions that inspire us, we shift our mind's inner soundtrack. It moves from grumbling about 'should', 'have to' and obligations to feeling excited about 'might', 'could' and possibilities.

On a physical level, you are creating new neurological pathways in your brain. These help to create new thought processes and habits that support shifts in all areas of your life.

You are effectively over-writing the old auto-pilot scripts that kept you stuck behaving in ways that are now out-of-date. You are giving your unconscious mind – the bit that runs the show – the clear message that inspiration is great and you'd like to experience more of feeling inspired.

This re-tunes your mind's radar to spot things that can inspire you – and miracles and synchronicities appear.

How might this help you create the future you've been dreaming of?

Every decision we make is based on either love or fear.

Fear-based choices tell us that change is terrifying and it could all go wrong.

Love-based choices tell us that we can make the shifts we need, to move towards where we want to be, and that it will probably be better than ok.

Decisions based on fear – worrying about what might go wrong and avoiding the worst case scenario – keep us stuck in old habits, out-of-date beliefs, jobs we hate and even relationships that have run their course.

Decisions based on love allow us to expand and grow, to become who we really are and to live life to the full.

Even though it might feel scary, it's never too late to make another choice.

And if you ask yourself whether that choice is from love or fear, the answer might surprise you – and it might just change that decision, if you let it!

Is there a love-based decision you could make today that your future you will thank you for?

It's impossible to think unhappy thoughts and do unhappy things, but to feel happy inside.

Mind and body are linked. Our thoughts trigger the body's chemical reactions that create our experience of our emotions and influence our physical well-being.

Think an angry thought and you'll feel angry – and your body will receive messages that tell it to do what it does, when you're feeling angry – including flooding your system with adrenalin and engaging your sympathetic nervous system's 'fight or flight' response. Choose a happy, uplifting thought and your body balances things out with your parasympathetic nervous system's relaxation and flow.

You don't need to aim to leap from angry to blissful. The most important thought you can choose is one that produces a feeling of relief and you've already turned things around. All it takes is choice – then practice and patience. But it will transform your experience of life.

Are there some happy thoughts that are begging to be let out to play?

Other people's 'stuff' and drama is just that.

Just because someone is wearing their 'stuff' and drama for all to see, it doesn't mean you have to join in with it. You don't have to pick that baggage up and help them carry it. You certainly don't have to wear it as your own.

You don't have to feed it. It's in no way your responsibility, no matter what they say.

It's not your 'stuff'. It's theirs.

Of course, you might want to help them, if they want to be helped. But that's very different from taking on their pain and emotions – and dancing their dance.

If you have to spend time with someone who is throwing their story around, you could imagine yourself being surrounded by a ball of beautiful light, so that their pain and fear bounces straight off.

Imagine cutting the invisible ties you might have to their story. Send them compassion.

It's their stuff, not yours.

Is there someone around you whose 'stuff' and drama you have been carrying? Is it time to put it down?

The first step towards changing is to accept how things are, right now.

We can't change something we are rejecting. As Carl Jung famously told us, what you resist persists. If you battle against something you don't like, you're giving it all of your attention and you're giving it power over how you feel.

And if what we want to change is one of our habits or beliefs, then rejecting it would mean we were rejecting part of who we are. Accept whatever it is. Let go of judging it. It doesn't mean it's acceptable. But it's here. It's part of your current experience. And it will remain so, for as long as you fight it.

Instead, how about connecting with whatever it is. If it's a 'biggie', you might like to see a 'you' in the mirror, connecting with it instead. Allow a sense of peace to wash through you and that situation or habit. Allow a sense of courage and strength to wash through. Allow a sense of deep acceptance to wash through. Now, what do you want instead? And when you've figured that out:

What action will you take today to allow that change to happen?

Want a magic wand for worrying?

Esther Hicks says that "Worrying is a way of creating a future you don't want." We put our effort, energy and actions into worrying about those worries or trying to avoid them. The funny thing about worrying is that it never fixes anything. It's a habit that many of us are addicted to, but it just breeds more worries.

When we're worrying, we get stuck in our heads, going over and over and round and round the thing that may never happen. The problem is that worrying about it means we're giving it so much attention that we actually make it more likely to happen.

So what can we do instead? Get active! If you spot yourself worrying, take a moment to stop and ask yourself: "What could I do differently, so that this is no longer an issue? Is there an action I could take?"

If it's something outside of your control then it's time to shift your perspective, so you can move to a place of acceptance. But if it's something you can do something about then taking a step towards a solution can remove a huge weight from your shoulders.

Is it time to let go of worrying today?

The other person's criticism could be the greatest gift you ever receive.

If someone criticises you, they're not feeling happy inside. Happy people don't lay into others. But if criticism really stings, then it means it's probably got a message for you.

If you were to use that criticism as a chance to look in the mirror – with compassionate honesty – it might be your chance to release an old habit that is ready and waiting to go.

To see whether there's a behaviour waiting to be released, you could ask yourself: "What am I thinking or believing about myself, which allows those words to cause me pain?"

Let the answer bubble up – it might not be what you're expecting. The answer has the potential to set you free from out-of-date beliefs and habits. Be gentle with yourself over this. The first step towards change is accepting how things currently are. The second step is taking inspired compassionate action.

Are you ready to feel the relief of accepting things, just as they are, in this moment?

You don't have to dance, if you don't want to. And it's ok to choose who to dance with.

If being around a particular person is feeling uncomfortable, it's ok to say no. And if you're not able to avoid them, you can still choose not to do the 'dance'. Rather than allowing yourself to get dragged into their drama and emotions – their need for your relationship to run in a particular way, for you to do and say what they need you to. You can choose to step back, to set boundaries – even if they're just in your mind.

When you are clear about what you feel is acceptable and what is not, it's much easier for you to make decisions, based on that and setting compassionate, firm boundaries. And, with practice, you'll find it easier to tell them about it.

It's not about rejecting the other person. It's about accepting that you can't change them and that the only way you can shift the situation is for you to do different steps in the dance. If you respond differently to them, it will change the dynamics and set you free from the old patterns.

Is there a dance you've been dancing whose routine needs to shift today?

Happiness starts one thought at a time.

If you're feeling down and you want to feel better, it can feel overwhelming. All that stuff about 'positive thinking' can feel impossible, when your mind is racing with worry and stress. The idea of making all your thoughts positive becomes an unreachable goal.

Yet all you ever need to do is to sort out the thought that you're currently thinking – right now. That's it. And you don't even need to get rid of it or change it. Simply stop feeding it, if it means you feel bad. We feed our thoughts with stories, by giving them our attention. If there's a thought that's dragging you down, choose to gently let go of feeding it. It will then melt away, naturally, without you having to do anything.

Next, consciously choose a thought that makes you feel even just a tiny bit better. You can do it. Think of someone you love; a happy memory; something you're enjoying; gratitude that you can breathe! Nurture that thought. Feed it. Let it grow. Then choose another. And another. One at a time.

This is your ladder to feeling happier.

Does today's drama really matter? Or would life be more fun, if you let it go?

When 'stuff' happens, it's easy to get stuck in the story our mind tells us. It whips up powerful emotions and wrecks our mood.

Feeding the drama can give us a short-term adrenalin rush, to which many of us are addicted, but it comes at a price. It impacts our happiness. The mind-body link means it impacts our physical health. It trains our mind to hunt out – and it will find it – more drama and more situations that stress us out.

But will today's drama really matter in ten years' time? What would the 'future you' advise? This is a question for your deeper wisdom to answer, not your inner drama queen…

If it's a yes, take some action. Then let the situation go. Perhaps even imagine cutting the invisible ties you have to it. **If it's a no**, then just let it go. Cut those ties. Allow yourself to move on to happier stuff. Life is too precious to let today's drama impact your future.

Is it time to benefit from that future hindsight and wisdom, today?

Is your 'but' wrecking your relationships?

There's a 3-lettered word that can cause havoc with your relationships, whether with work colleagues or with those we love at home.

But...

We think we're being positive and then we add in a 'but'. There's a problem with this. The mind is hard-wired to expect bad news after a 'but'. It negates the message that came before it.

"Your presentation was great, but..."
"The main course was lovely, but..."
"Your dress is a great colour, but..."

Notice how these sentences feel? It produces an emotional reaction and also a physical reaction – often a tightening in the stomach area and a shift in the shoulders.. Using 'but' is a habit many of us have. We use it to link two ideas in a sentence, without realising it's popped in – and we usually don't need it.

What can you use instead? **And...**

Play with the sentences above using 'and'. Notice how different it feels?

Would you like to play with 'and' today and see what shifts?

Happiness isn't about the destination. It's about how you live the journey.

In each and every moment, we can choose *how* to experience the journey of life. We can choose to have a sad journey; an angry journey; a grumpy journey; a happy journey. It changes with each and every thought, triggering emotions in our bodies.

The magic of life means that if we realise we're not on the kind of journey we want to be on we can make minor shifts to the thoughts we're feeding, to get back on track. We get what we focus on. If we look for problems, we'll find problems. If we look for drama, we'll find drama. If we look for opportunities to help and serve others, that's what we'll find.

Changing your experience of life's journey is as simple as choosing another thought – one that brings a sense of relief; one that helps you to feel more positive. One thought at a time. All you need to do is to set your intention to enjoy the journey.

Are there any tweaks you'd like to make to your journey today?

If they're getting to you, remember to use your mirror ball!

If you're stuck in a situation where people are behaving in a way that leads to you feeling bad, there's a simple technique you can use that will transform your experience.

The first thing to remember is that the other person's difficult behaviour isn't really about you. It's coming from their inner pain and drama. Don't take it on as your 'stuff'. Then, rather than being dragged into their drama and pain, imagine you are surrounded by a giant sparkly mirror ball.

This mirror ball bounces back and protects you from anything that hasn't come from a place of peace or love, which isn't intended for your personal growth. It also reflects back to you anything you send out that isn't coming from positive intentions and love, so you can learn from it. In this way, you can interact with the 'difficult person' without getting into the emotions. And it helps you to respond with compassion.

Is it time to dust off your mirror ball?

When was the last time you actually experienced life, as you were living it?

How often are you actually 'here'? How much of our time do we spend worrying about the past or fretting about the future? When was the last time you tasted your tea?

One of the biggest epidemics in our Western lifestyle is that of not being present – not being 'here' – being anywhere else but in this moment. Our life is lived through our minds.

Coming back to the present moment is essential if you want to reclaim your power to take action and make changes in your life. You can't make changes in the past – it's done and dusted. You can't make changes in the future – it's not here yet. This precious moment is the only time you have. And **it's where your life is waiting for you**.

Coming back to this moment can help you get out of 'auto-pilot' mode and make fresh choices. It shifts life from the treacle experience to one of ease and lightness.

Want to come home? Take a deep sighing breath and say: "I am here."

We change our experience of life by changing the way we look at the world.

We experience life through the filters of our past worries, future stresses and current 'to do' lists. But none of this is real. It's all just stories we tell ourselves. Living life through those filters is stressful and means we're missing out on most of the pleasure and fun; taking life too seriously.

Bring yourself back to your physical body, out of your thinking mind, for a moment. Notice what you notice. Notice the physical sensations. Let your awareness rest on your breath.

It's time to bring your awareness back from the past, the future, the 'maybes', into this present moment. When we do this, it's common to feel a sense of relief; a lessening of stresses and often an awareness of the deeper peace and wisdom that are always inside us.

Now imagine whatever you're due to do next today, but first coming back to this moment – to that sense of relief and peace. How have things shifted?

Are you ready to change the way you look at the world today?

If you get into the 'gap' between the stimulus and your response, you will change your world.

Most of what we do runs on auto-pilot. It's not a bad thing. It's useful to be able to remember how to make a cup of tea or get dressed, without having to figure it out anew each time.

But some of those auto-pilot scripts get out-dated. We cling to them, like beloved old friends, but they eventually create problems.

You can spot them when you find yourself reacting particularly strongly to something someone has said or done. It's a sign that it's time to get into the 'gap'.

By bringing your awareness out of your thinking mind and into the present moment, you can slip into that split-second gap between the stimulus (someone's behaviour) and your response. When you catch yourself about to react, take a calming breath and ask yourself: "Which response would my deeper wisdom choose, right now?" And watch how your world changes.

Is it time to get into the 'gap' today?

You can only make a choice if you have awareness.

Are you running around on auto-pilot, thrown about on an ocean full of emotions and habits like an inflatable dinghy in a storm?

The problem is that it means we react to situations with our pre-programmed old habits and beliefs. We rarely spot what's really going on and we tend to live on adrenalin, as we fire-fight our way from one stress to the next.

We might be enjoying our projection of the 'facts', telling the story 'our way' in our head.

But if we're wandering around half-asleep and unaware of our behaviours and the choices we're making, we are unlikely to end up where we want to be. We keep going round in circles and miss the opportunities that line our path.

Bringing your awareness back to the 'here and now' at random points during your day is all it takes to create the habit of awareness. The gift this awareness brings you is giving you back your choice over your thoughts, habits and emotions.

How could you remind yourself to experiment with awareness today?

Are you ready to get out of your 'story head'?

Most of us, most of the time, are sleep-walking through life, stuck in our 'story heads'.

We don't notice the proverbial daffodils, because our story head is too busy retelling the latest drama. We convince ourselves that we're too busy to smell those roses, because our story head reminds us of everything else there is to do. We spot the annoying or unkind things that people do, because our story head points them out to us. **We end up living life through our stories, not our senses.**

Our story head tells us that it's more important to stress about whether or not an overdue email has arrived or how last week's presentation went, rather than really connecting with those we love and experiencing the beauty of the world around us. Is that how you want things to be? Here's a question you can ask yourself, to shift things:

"Do I want to live this experience through my story head or would I rather enjoy what's real, in this moment?" Then take inspired action!

Are you fed up of not having enough time?

"I don't have enough time!" is a mantra that many of us have engraved on our hearts. We end up rushing through life, stressed and exhausted, always convincing ourselves that time is too short.

But time can race and time can slow. Much of it is down to our perception.

If we come back to the present moment, we can set ourselves free from the mind's worries about time; we can get one thing done and dusted, before we move on to the next; we can pause the 'time-poor stories' we normally tell ourselves.

And we can shift our attitude, with a simple gratitude mantra:

How about choosing new perspective? Instead of focusing on not having enough time, how about telling yourself:

"I am thankful for the time I have."

Try it now. How different does that feel? Notice the shift?

How might being thankful for the time you have help you today?

Is it time to stop carrying around so many heavy rocks?

Have you noticed how many of us are carrying heavy rocks around with us, in the form of grudges, resentments and pain from the past?

Sometimes the weight of these rocks is so much that we feel we can't go on carrying them, yet we still manage. It can leave us feeling exhausted and it's robs us of life's light-heartedness and fun. It uses up our energy and means there's nothing left for jumping at life's amazing opportunities.

But the secret that nobody tells us is that carrying those old rocks is optional – it's our choice. We can choose whether or not to keep carrying them. Right now, you could select a rock and choose to put it down. Perhaps you might like to imagine yourself doing that now?

As you put the rock down, how about lovingly forgiving yourself for ever picking up that rock? How about seeing the invisible ties that kept you carrying it being cut and filled with love? Now take a step or ten into the future and see that the old rock is where it belongs – in your past.

How does it feel, to put down those rocks today?

Could you become a 'spreader of sunshine'?

Getting stuck in our problems and worries leads to feeling bad – and that rarely fixes anything.

Plus it's contagious. Spend ten minutes in a room with someone stuck in a miserable drama and you know what it will do to your mood.

But if we set our mind's radar to look for opportunities to spread sunshine and an upbeat mood, we will find them. It will change the world around us – and our experience of life.

There's no technique more powerful than this for shifting your life. No matter how bad you are feeling, if you choose to look for ways to help others to feel better, it comes back to you in bucket-loads.

Even if your smile or positive attitude impacts just one person today, that's still a heart that has been lifted – a life that has been shifted. And you never know where that ripple effect might go.

Whose ray of sunshine could you be today?

What's Next?

Please make the most of *The Little Book Of Daily Sunshine*'s bonus resources. You'll find them and Clare Josa's free monthly newsletter at:

www.DailySunshine.co.uk/bonus

Connect with Clare Josa on Facebook:

www.Facebook.com/cjosa/

You could take part in one of Clare's online life-changing courses:

www.ClareJosa.com/Online-Courses/

You could join in one of her face-to-face workshops:

www.ClareJosa.com/Workshops/

You could discover her other books and CDs:

www.ClareJosa.com/Clare-Josa-Books-CDs/

Above all, please make a commitment to your future happiness and choose actions today that help you to love every moment of this wondrous journey of life!

About Clare Josa

Clare Josa speaks and teaches internationally on how changing the world isn't about what you *do*, it's about who you allow yourself to *become*.

She has been mentoring Business Leaders and Passionate World-Changers since 2002. As an entrepreneur herself, the creator of over fifteen years of online and face-to-face training courses, and the author of six published books, she knows about the hidden blocks that keep us stuck, dreaming big, but playing small. She has been through most of them, herself.

But she also knows how to get past them. That's why she wrote The Little Book Of Daily Sunshine for you, so you could do it, too.

She originally trained as an engineer (she has a Master's Degree in Mechanical Engineering And German), but she is also an NLP Trainer (practical psychology) and a certified Meditation & Yoga teacher. She loves demystifying Ancient Wisdom into practical actions you can take to change your life in less time than it takes to boil a kettle. Her clients call it 'engineer-approved woo-woo'. And it all comes with a bucket load of common sense and a generous dollop of humour.

You can find thousands of inspirational articles, videos, podcast episodes and practical life-changing techniques – as well as her free monthly newsletter – over at her website:

www.clarejosa.com

Message From The Author:

I really hope you enjoyed *The Little Book Of Daily Sunshine*. If you did, please could you leave a review wherever you bought it (or on Amazon) letting people know why you liked it? It helps more readers to find the book! And you can let my team know by emailing hello@clarejosa.com. I would love to hear from you.

Other Books By Clare Josa

Dare To Dream Bigger: ISBN 9781908854797

Dare To Dream Bigger distils 15+ years of mentoring entrepreneurs and passionate world-changers into exercises you can do at home, in your PJs, to *get out of your own way*.

If you're fed up with dreaming big, but playing small, then it's time to clear out those hidden blocks, so you can make the difference you are *really* here to make.

And Dare To Dream Bigger guides you step by step through how to 'be the change' you wish to see.

52 Mindful Moments: ISBN 9781908854445

Want to feel less stressed, happier, calmer and more at peace, but you don't have the time?

What if all it took to change your life was one mindful minute? Could you spare that long?

The inspirational mindfulness techniques in 52 Mindful Moments will help you to shift away from feeling stressed, worried and exhausted, to feeling calmer, happier, more at peace and more alive, in under sixty seconds.

A Year Full Of Gratitude:

ISBN 978-1908854773

We've all heard about how gratitude can change your life. But where on earth do you start? And how do you create the habit if your thinking mind is making you feel miserable?

A Year Full Of Gratitude combines a gratitude journal with a year-long course, to help you retrain your monkey mind to think thoughts that make you feel happier, taming your inner critic and helping you to smile for no reason!

All of Clare Josa's books are available to order from local bookstores and from major online retailers.

Made in United States
Orlando, FL
15 October 2022